MAKING MODEL AEROPLANES

If you had been alive a hundred years ago you would probably never have ridden a bicycle, you would certainly never have had a ride in a car and if someone had told you that he wanted to fly like a bird you would have thought he was a dreamer with his head in the clouds but his feet planted firmly on the ground.

All this was soon to change. In 1903 the Wright brothers made four powered flights. Man could at last fly like the birds.

MAKING MODEL AEROPLANES shows you how to make some of these early planes like the *Antoinette VII* and the *Bleriot XI* as well as aeroplanes used in the Second World War like the *Spitfire*.

Other books by Peter Fairhurst

MAKING MODEL RACING CARS
MAKING MODEL CARS
MAKING MODEL WARTIME VEHICLES

all published by CAROUSEL BOOKS

Peter Fairhurst

MAKING MODEL AEROPLANES

CAROUSEL BOOKS
A DIVISION OF TRANSWORLD PUBLISHERS LTD

MAKING MODEL AEROPLANES

A CAROUSEL BOOK 0 552 54099 4

First publication in Great Britain

PRINTING HISTORY
Carousel edition published 1976
Carousel edition reprinted 1976
Carousel edition reprinted 1978
Carousel edition reprinted 1983

Carousel Books are published by
Transworld Publishers Ltd.,
Century House, 61-63 Uxbridge Road,
Ealing, London W5 5SA
Made and printed in Great Britain by
The Guernsey Press Co. Ltd., Guernsey, Channel Islands.

CONTENTS

Introduction

This book contains the instructions and plans required to build models of twelve aeroplanes. Two of the planes chosen are from the very early years of aviation and helped to prove that powered flight could be a practical means of transport. Several of the models are of planes that established the aeroplane as a military vehicle during the First World War. There is a model of a development of the first sea plane and a model of the first aeroplane to fly solo from New York to Paris. The remaining models are of aeroplanes used during the Second World War, two fighters and one reconnaisance plane.

The models are all built to the same scale 1 : 48, which means that each foot of the original plane is represented by $\frac{1}{4}$in of the model or that 1 cm represents 48 cms. The technique and materials used make the models less detailed than the plastic kits on the market but with care and patience you should be able to produce an excellent scale model and have the satisfaction of displaying something which is *all your own work.*

It will take you several hours to make each model and, for the first ones at least, you should make sure that you follow the instructions very carefully. When you have finished your first models you will understand the techniques much better and be able to make a very good job of the more difficult ones. The easiest models are marked * and the most difficult ones are marked xx.

Remember, read the instructions carefully, more than once, if necessary, and make sure you understand each stage in the construction. Don't rush the work, the patience and care you put into it will be shown in the finished model.

Here is a list of the models you can make with a guide to how difficult or easy each one is:

xx	Bleriot XI	France 1909
*	Antoinette VI	France 1909
	Curtiss Flying Boat	U.S.A. 1914
xx	Be 2a	Britain 1914
xx	Nieuport 17	France 1916
	Fokker EIII	Germany 1915
	Fokker Dr I	Germany 1918
xx	Sopwith Pup	Britain 1918
*	Ryan NYP	U.S.A. 1927
*	Piper Grasshopper	U.S.A. WWII
	Messerschmitt Bf. 109 E	Germany WWII
	Supermarine 'Spitfire'	Britain WWII

—1—

If you had been alive a hundred years ago you would probably never have ridden a bicycle, you would certainly never have had a ride in a car and if someone had told you that he wanted to fly like a bird you would have thought he was a dreamer with his head in the clouds but his feet planted firmly on the ground.

All this was soon to change. The industrial revolution was in full swing and machinery of all types was being invented and developed. In the 1880's the bicycle became a practical means of transport. In the 1890's the motor car was in its infancy and growing up very quickly and the first ten years of the twentieth century saw man's dream of centuries realized, he could, at last, fly like the birds.

For hundreds of years man had envied the birds but we will take up the story in 1891 when Otto Lilienthal became the first man to fly with wings. This German Engineer had studied birds in flight and built a glider based on the shape of their wings.

From then, until he crashed to his death in 1896, he made over 2,000 successful and safe glides. During this time he published several papers on his work and fired the imagination of many would-be 'flyers' who began experimenting with machines of their own.

Lilienthal's death stunned the European movement and no significant advances were made for many years. Meanwhile, in America, two brothers, Wilbur and Orville Wright had started building a series of models and then full size gliders to test their theories. Their interest was not so much in flying but in the science behind it. They believed that, by studying everything that had been written about flying from a scientific point of view and then building models designed on their findings, they would solve the problems of flight. They were convinced that most existing aeronautical theories were wrong, and dangerous and, in fact, did much of their experimental work in the world's first wind tunnel.

Perhaps the biggest reason that no one had, so far, built a successful powered machine was that there had been no suitable source of power available before the turn of the century. With the development of the motor car engine into a powerful, reliable and lightweight power plant, that reason was about to be removed.

The Wright brothers ran a cycle manufacturing business in Dayton, Ohio, which gave them the advantage of the facilities and engineering skills necessary for their plane building. In 1903 the brothers decided to apply power to their No. 4 glider. They designed their own engine, based on a good automobile unit, and it was built by their machinist in the workshop in about 6 weeks. The engine was mounted in the centre of the biplane and drove two propellers by chains and sprockets, behind the main wings, to push the aircraft.

On the 17th December, 1903, the Wright brothers flew themselves into history: they made four powered flights on that day, the longest being 852 feet in 59 seconds. Over the next two years they improved their

design and by 1905 had a machine, the Wright Flyer III, that could be controlled successfully. In October of that year Orville flew a distance of over 20 miles and, the following day, Wilbur covered almost 25 miles.

News of the Wrights' achievements was slow in crossing the Atlantic where most people still thought of flying as an impossible dream. The first man to fly in Europe was Alberto Santos-Dumont, a Brazilian living in Paris, who had built and flown 14 motor driven airships from 1878 to 1906. He then built a very large box kite with fuselage running forward to support a tail assembly and an engine in the rear.

He launched this 'back to front' aeroplane from underneath his airship and flew it safely to the ground. During the next few weeks Santos-Dumont took off from the ground and made several successful, though short, flights.

Several other pioneers flew in Europe at about this time but none of them had real control of their machines. The power that their engines developed was largely wasted because the propellers were very inefficient. With no experience to fall back on, determination and luck were the main ingredients of a successful, and usually short, flight.

In 1908 the Wrights' Flyer was demonstrated in France and the world realized that flying was a reality. Wilbur spent several months in Europe and during that time made many long flights during which his machine was under complete control at all times. The European pioneers flew like a hen fluttering along chased by a dog. Wilbur Wright flew like a bird with graceful banks and turns.

These demonstrations were the stimulus to renewed attempts by the pioneers. The Wright brothers' influence was to revolutionize European aviation.

The reborn interest in flying was probably strongest in France where numerous successful machines were developed and during 1909 great progress was made. Many of these machines were based on the Wrights' design, a biplane with forward elevator and pusher propellers. Other machines were of the tractor monoplane type, a single wing with elevator in the rear and the propeller pulling from the front.

Flying was, by this time, accepted as a practical means of transport and the next few years saw tremendous advances in the design and construction of aeroplanes. European aviation now led the world. The military applications of the aeroplane were soon recognized. To be able to fly over enemy lines and report troop positions and movements would be a great help in the event of war, and planes were designed for this purpose.

With the outbreak of the First World War the aeroplane proved itself invaluable not only as a scout but also as a fighting machine. Even greater advances were made; planes became more powerful, faster, more manoeuvrable and safer. They were fitted with guns and some carried bombs.

When the war was over the new aircraft industry

turned its attention to passenger carrying and commercial aviation, and once again planes became bigger and more powerful. Flights across the Atlantic became possible and soon airlines were operating services to all parts of the world.

The Second World War saw the re-birth of the fighter aircraft and the development of the big bombers. By 1945 we had the jet engine which heralded a new era in aviation, both civil and military. In less than 50 years the aeroplane had developed from a flimsy construction of bamboo or steel tubes, tensioned with wire and covered with canvas which could fly only a short distance at about 30–40 mph, into a very sophisticated machine capable of flying at great speed over long distances with absolute accuracy and in weather conditions that would have made any sort of flight impossible in those early years.

Making the Models

The basic method of making all the models in the book is the same and is explained in this section.

All the parts needed to make each plane are printed **the correct size** in the following pages but they must be transferred to thin card for the models. Read through the instructions carefully and study the plans for a few minutes so that you understand how the various parts fit together to make the model.

Some of the models are more complicated than others and if you make one of the easier ones first you will soon master the technique and find that the others are not too difficult. The easier ones are marked *. (See page 7.)

To build the models you will need:

Tools

Sharp pencil/ball point pen.
Ruler
Compass
Scissors – (medical scissors are excellent).
Craft knife.

Materials

Card (thin card or thick drawing paper).
Carbon paper
Glue – white PVA is probably the best
Wood – balsa $\frac{1}{4}$in × $\frac{1}{16}$in (6mm × 1.5 mm)
cocktail sticks or $\frac{1}{16}$in (1.5mm) dowel.
Cotton
Thick card for wheels
Paint – Acrylic/Polymer colours
Varnish. Polymer varnish is ideal.

Stage A

You must first transfer the plans from the book on to the card. Place the card and a piece of carbon paper under the plan and hold firmly in position.

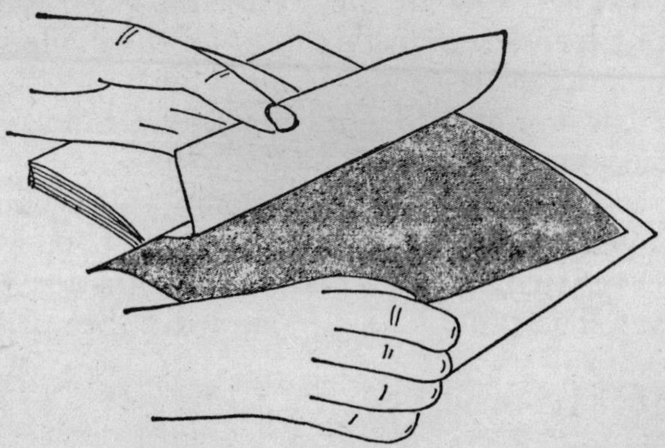

Using the point of the compass prick a hole at each end of all the straight lines.

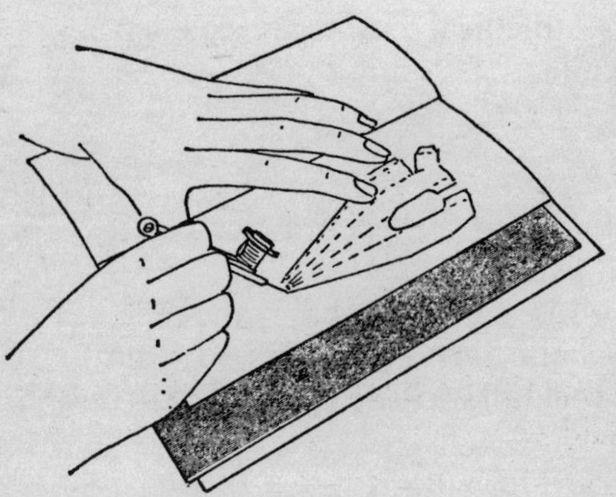

With the pencil or pen draw carefully over all the curved lines.

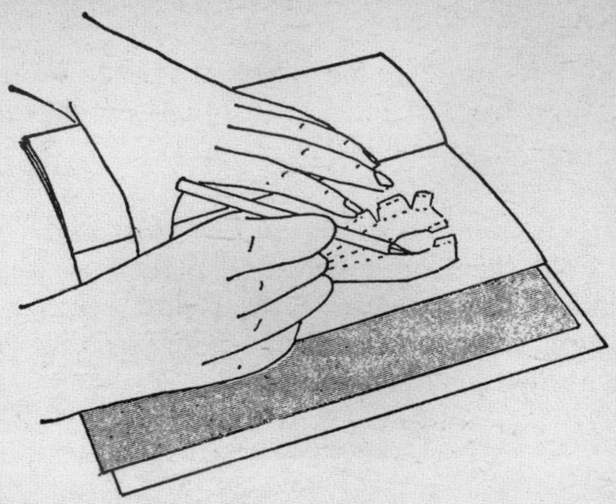

Again with compass, prick all the dots on each part. These are the positions for struts, bracing wires, etc., and they should be enlarged to the required size during assembly. Remove the card and join up all the dots.

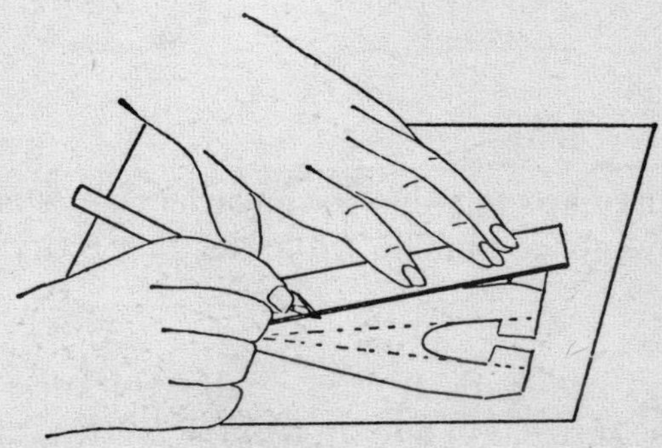

Check with the plan to see that you have not made any mistakes.

Stage B

Score along all the folding lines.

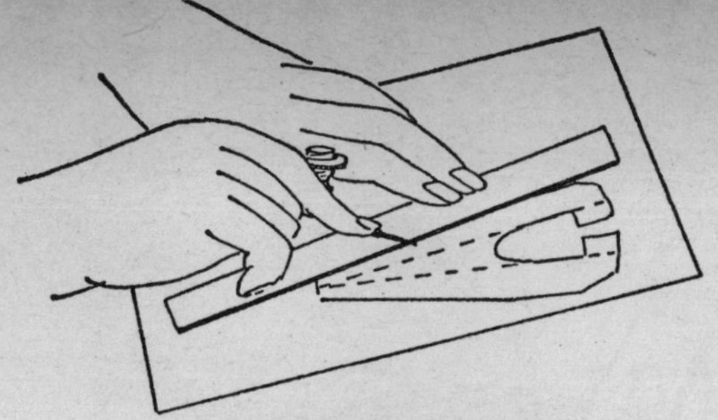

Then cut out the pieces with scissors and/or craft knife. Fold the scored lines and make sure that you understand how to assemble each part before you attempt to glue it. When you are quite sure that you are ready, apply the adhesive carefully.

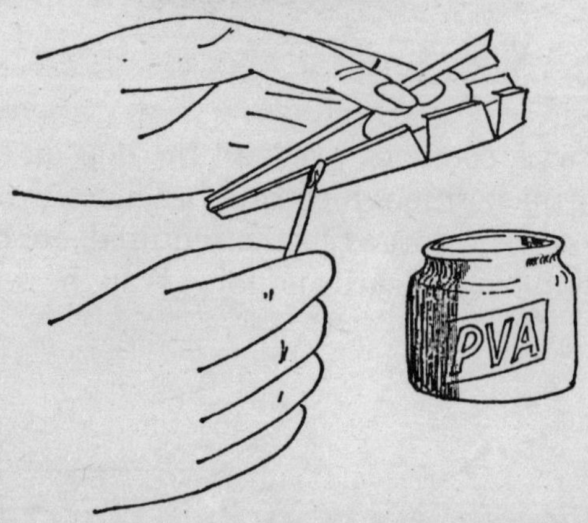

Stick the parts together in the order suggested. Make sure the joints do not slip while the glue is drying.

Stage C

The wings are made from a double thickness of card to give them strength and an aerofoil section, a piece of balsa wood $\frac{1}{4}$in × $\frac{1}{16}$in (6mm × 1.5mm) is sandwiched between them. The wing should be cut out. Where there are two halves they should be joined together edge to edge with a narrow strip of card glued over the two pieces. The leading edge is made by the fold. Glue the balsa strip in position on the lower surface.

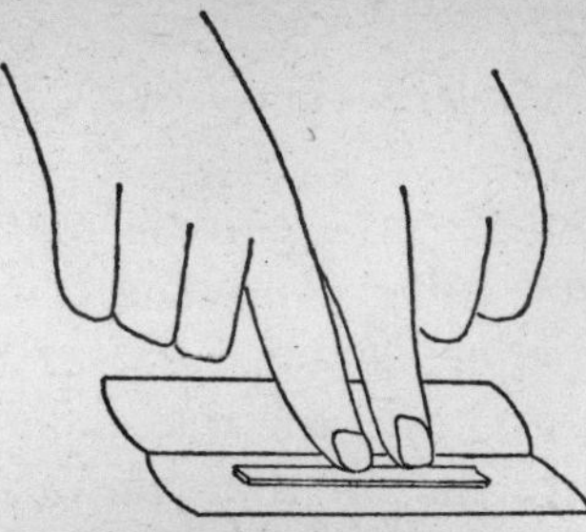

Apply a narrow strip of glue along the trailing edge and tips of the wing, fold over, press down and allow to dry. It may be necessary to trim the edges of the completed wing.

Some wings require slots or holes to locate the struts, these should be cut out before the wing is assembled.

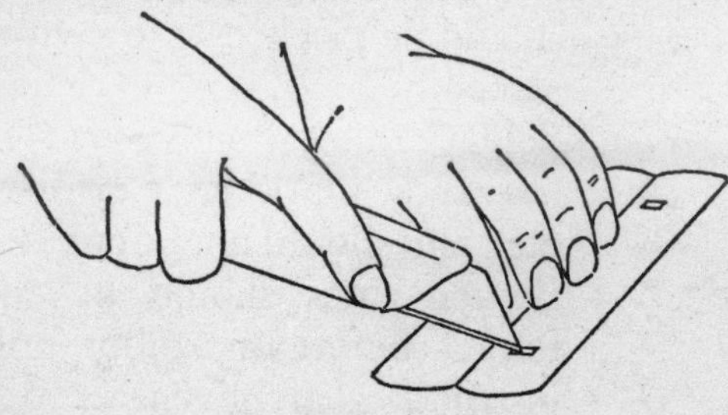

Stage D

Glue the various parts together in the order suggested and allow to dry. Make sure that all the parts are in the correct position.

Stage E

The undercarriage should be made from $\frac{1}{16}$in (1.5mm) dowel or cocktail sticks cut to length. In most cases the main struts are glued into holes (made with your compass again) in the body and you may find that binding with cotton will help to fix axles to them. Wheels should be cut from thicker card. Use dark cotton for bracing wires, thread a needle and use it to pass the cotton through the card.

Guns, propellers, etc., can be made from scraps of balsa, card or any other handy material.

Paint the model as indicated or choose your own colour scheme and add the markings by hand or using transfers. Where the original aircraft was painted the model should be varnished, fabric wings, etc., should be left dull.

Diagram Key

■ ● Represent positions of wing and undercarriage struts and should be cut out before assembly.

• Show positions of bracing wire and should be pricked with compass before assembly.

——— Solid outlines should be cut. Some solid lines show markings, elevators, ailerons, etc., and should not be cut.

- - - - - Broken lines should be scored and folded before assembly unless other instructions are given.

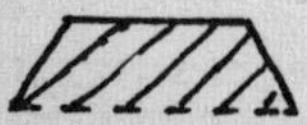

Represent tabs and should generally be glued.

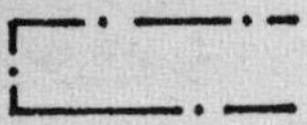

Shows the position of balsa strengtheners. These balsa strips are fitted inside the wing but are shown on the same surface as the markings which are on the outside. Mark the position with a small prick and then transfer the lines to the inside surface.

N.B. *Where only one half of a wing is shown two should be cut out but be sure to mark one for the left and the other for the right.*

xx Bleriot

Louis Bleriot was a French engineer with a flourishing business making searchlights and acetylene lamps for motor cars. He became actively interested in aviation in 1901–2 when he built model flying machines. In 1905 and 1906 he had a float glider and a powered aeroplane built for him but neither was very satisfactory.

In 1907 Bleriot built no less than three totally different monoplanes: The first, his *No. V*, never flew more than 6 metres; the second, *No. VI*, crash landed after a flight of 184 metres; and the third, *No. VII*, remained airborne for about 45 seconds, covering a distance of about 500 metres.

The *Bleriot VIII* of 1908 was a little more successful and was the basis of the design for the *No. XI* which became one of the most famous pioneers of aviation. It was in this aeroplane that Bleriot flew from France to England on Sunday, July 25th, 1909, to win the *Daily Mail* prize of £1,000 for the first powered flight across the English Channel.

The flight was remarkable, the aircraft was extremely fragile and grossly under-powered with its 3-cylinder 25hp Anzani engine, the weather was not very promising and Bleriot had neither maps nor a compass and had to walk on crutches as he had badly scalded his left foot on a recent flight. Nevertheless Louis Bleriot, determined to make the flight, climbed into his plane, asked his helpers the way to Dover and set off across the water in the direction of the English coast.

Within 40 minutes the pilot had won his place in history. At about ten past five on that Sunday morning Bleriot had conquered the Channel and clearly demonstrated that Britain was effectively no longer an island that could be defended by a mighty navy. With this flight, Bleriot had won not only the £1,000 prize but also the respect and admiration of the world. That day marked the turning point in aviation. Governments became aware that the aeroplane was no longer a plaything of the rich and the military applications were being considered.

The immediate result of Bleriot's historic flight was that he received orders for over 100 similar aircraft and the *type XI* in various modifications, became known the world over and remained in service as a reconnaissance and training machine well into World War I.

During the war Bleriot took over the Deperdussin works and developed the famous SPAD aircraft. The Company continued to be a major force in French aviation and was nationalized in 1937, a year after Bleriot's death.

The Bleriot XI **France 1909**

Power One 25hp Anzani fan-shaped, three-cylinder air-cooled engine driving a two-bladed wooden propeller 6ft 7in (2.00m) diameter.
Fuselage 26ft 3in (8.00m) long wire braced steel tube box girder with partially fabric-covered sides and wooden floor under the cockpit. Inside the body was an inflated rubber bag to keep the plane afloat if it came down in the water.
Wings Span 25ft 7in (7.80m). Area 150.7sq ft (14sq m) fabric-covered ash frame stiffened with aluminium and detachable to ease transport and storage. The wings were braced with wire to a steel pylon above the fuselage and to the wheel struts. The rear portion of the wings was flexible and could be warped by the pilot to give lateral control of the machine.

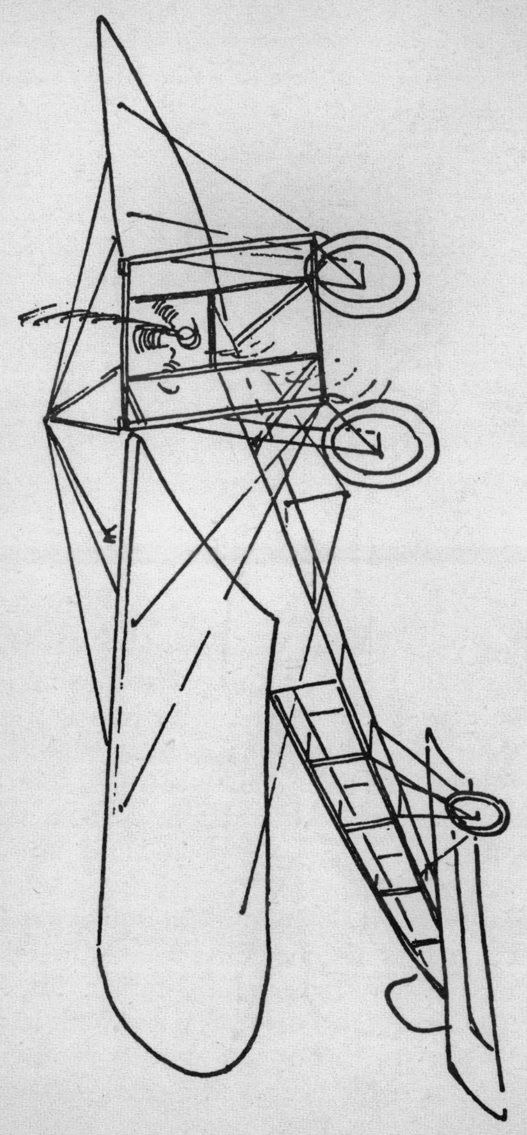

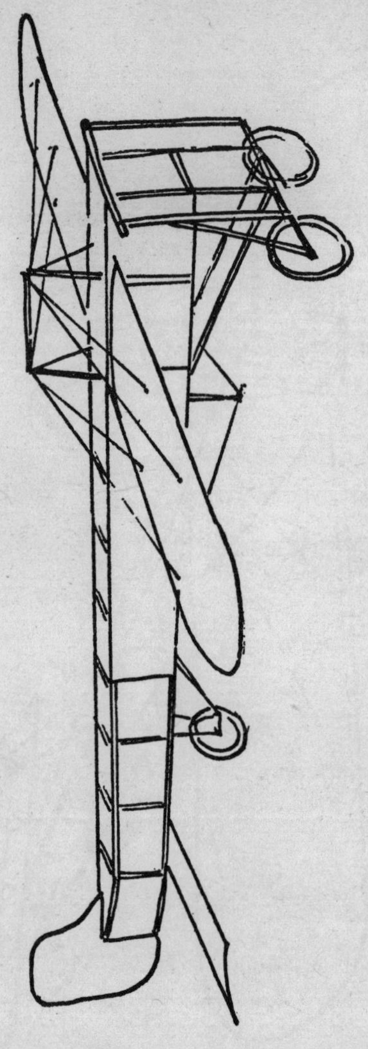

To Make the Bleriot XI

Follow the stages in the general instructions paying particular attention to the following details:

(1) The fuselage is made in the usual way; be sure to cut out the wing mounting position before assembly.

(2) The tabs at the rear of the fuselage are doubled over to strengthen the sides and the top and bottom are left open.

(3) The two sections of the rudder are glued together with the fuselage rear tabs sandwiched between them.

(4) The tailplane should be curved before the two surfaces are glued together, it is then mounted underneath the rear of the fuselage as shown.

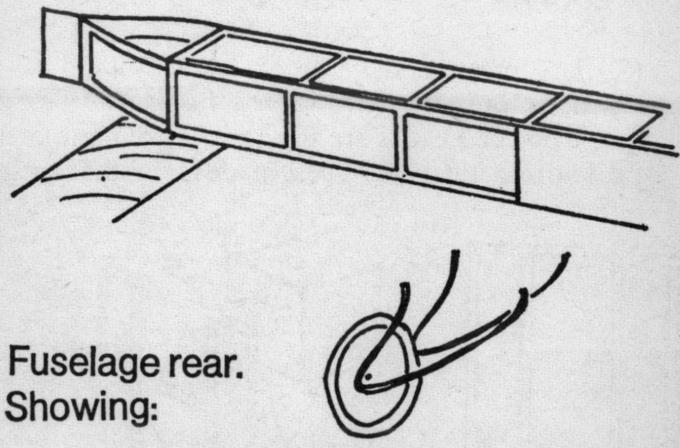

Fuselage rear.
Showing:

Tailplane mounted under fuselage.

Rear wheel 7/16″ (1.2 cm) diameter in frame made from thin wire.

Fuselage marking shown to represent open framework.

(5) The wings are quite straightforward but should be curved before gluing. The centre section should then be glued into the cut-out section on top of the fuselage.

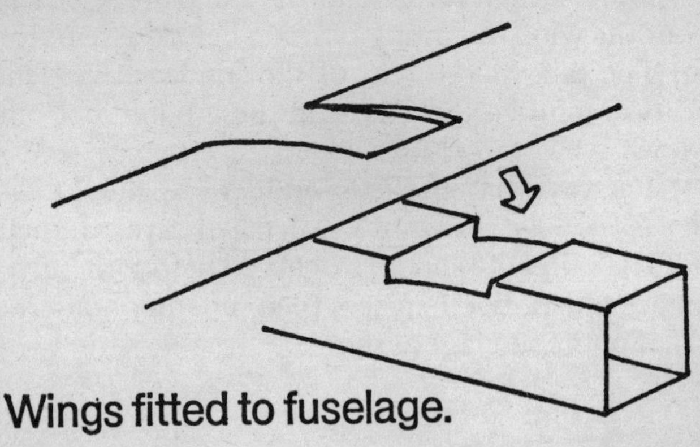

Wings fitted to fuselage.

(6) The undercarriage front frame should be assembled, before it is fixed to the fuselage, from $\frac{1}{16}$in (1.5mm) dowel. Details are shown in the diagram.

(7) The bracing pylon is best made from stiff bristle.

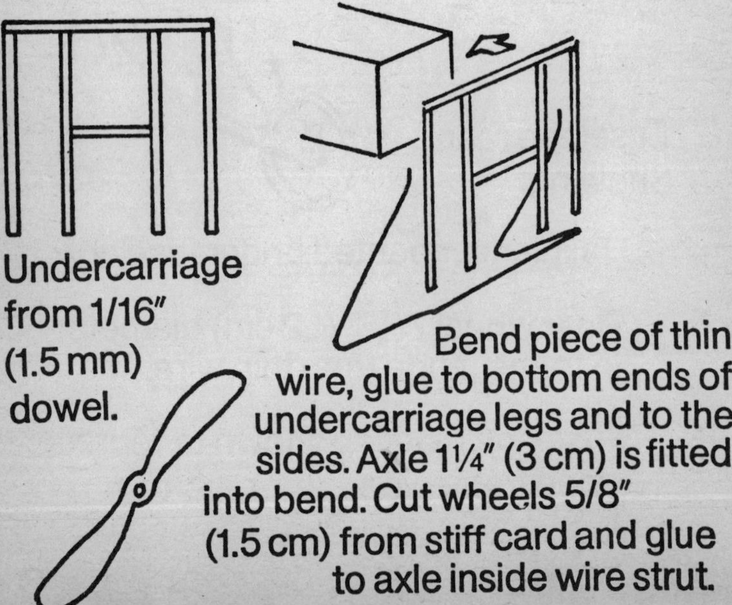

Model Plans

Fuselage.
Cut out for wing mounting.
Rudder Tailplane.
Tabs A doubled over leaving top and bottom of fuselage open.

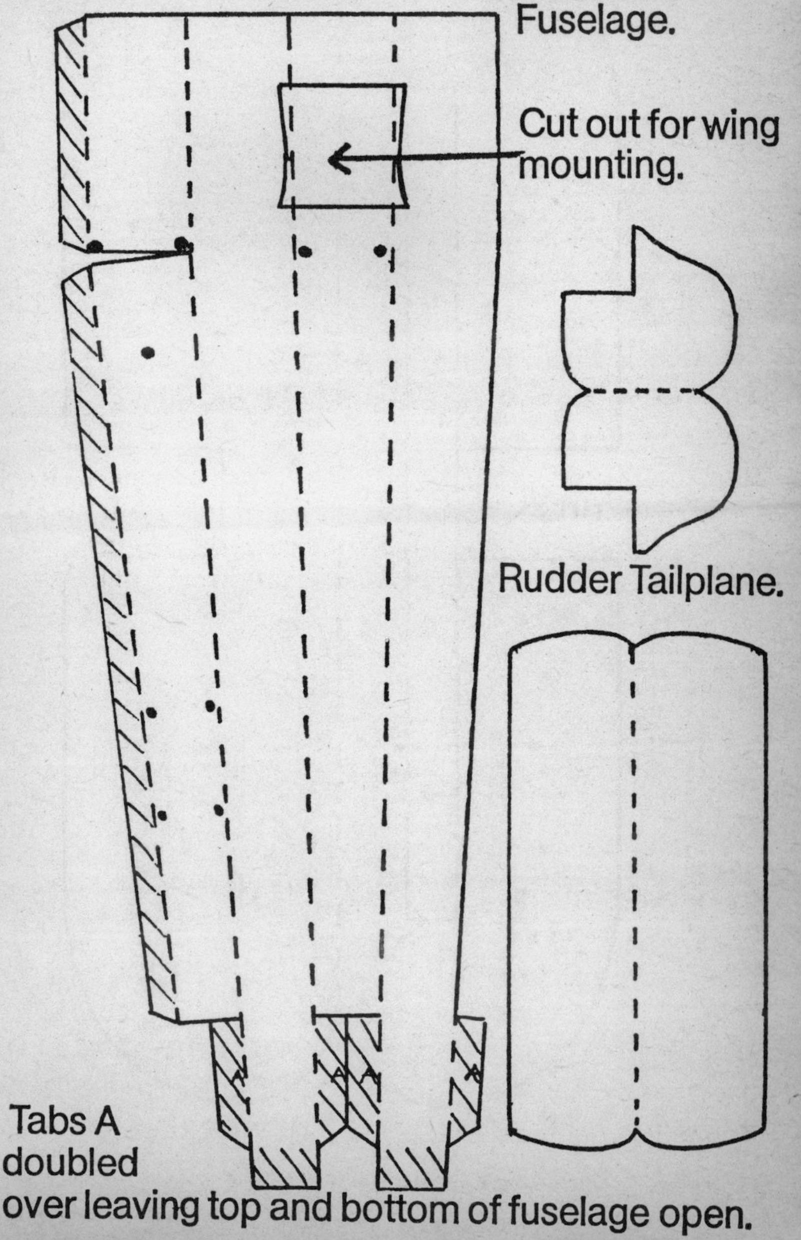

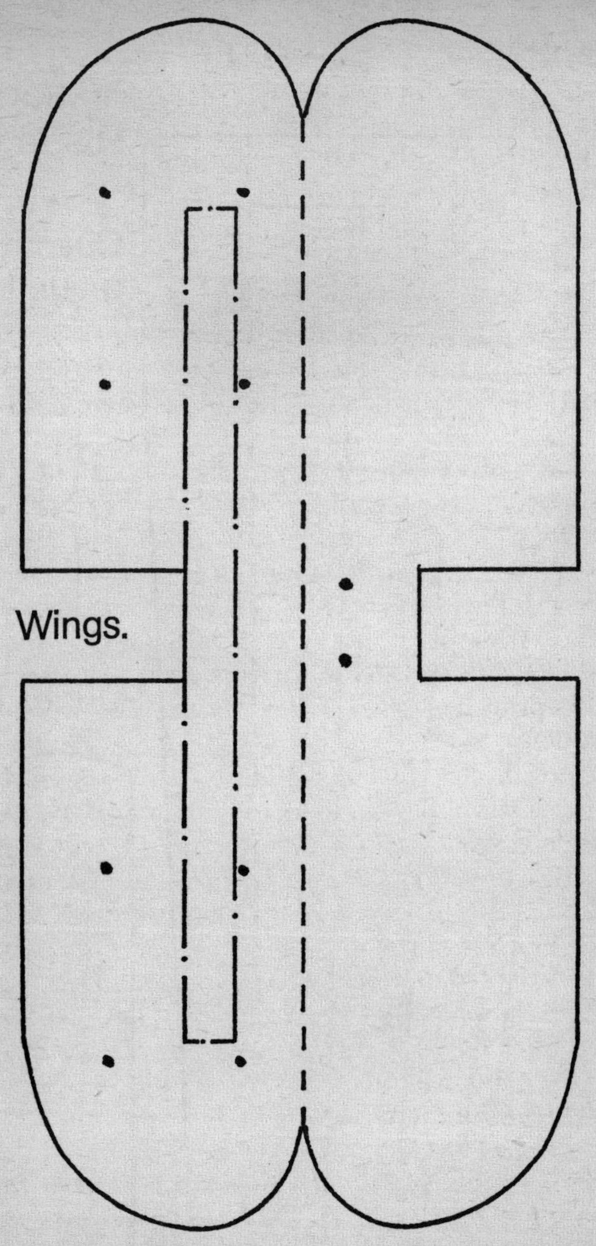
Wings.

*Antoinette

At the turn of the century a French company, the Société Antoinette, were producing an excellent range of engines designed to power motor boats. These Antoinette engines were to become very popular with pioneer aviators and were used in many early European aircraft.

The *Société Antoinette* was named after the daughter of the Company's Director, Jules Gastambide, but the leading figure was Leon Levavaseur, an Artist and Engineer, who was responsible for the company's early aircraft.

Levavaseur's first full size aeroplane was tested in 1903 and was a complete failure and his second was abandoned in 1908 when it was almost completed. Two more planes were built and tested at about this time and were a little more successful. The first of the classic Antoinette monoplanes was the *Antoinette IV* which first flew in October 1908 and, after several modifications and improvements during the winter, was prepared for an attempt to win the *Daily Mail* prize for the first cross-Channel flight. The flight ended with engine failure after 7½ miles and the pilot, Hubert Lathom, and the aeroplane were rescued from the sea. This flight was on the 19th July, 1909, and as Lathom was determined to make the first powered Channel crossing, he rushed to Paris to arrange for his new plane, the *Antoinette VII* to be delivered to the coast for his next attempt.

Lathom made his second Channel flight on the 27th July, 1909, but he had already lost the prize to Bleriot. It was the maiden flight of the new machine and, as before, had an unfortunate watery end when only one mile away from Dover.

Both Lathom's aircraft were rescued from the sea, rebuilt and flew again. At the Rheims Aviation meeting in August 1909, the first one flew 96 miles (155km) in 2 hours 17 minutes to win the second prize in the Grand Prix, and the second won the altitude prize at 508ft (155m).

The *Antoinette VII*, without doubt, was the most successful aeroplane of the year and formed the basis of a machine that was put into production.

Antoinette VII **France 1909**

Power One 50hp Antoinette water-cooled, Vee-type 8-cylinder engine driving a two-bladed aluminium and steel propeller 6ft 1in (1.85m) diameter.

Fuselage 37ft 9in (11.50m) long triangular ash and spruce airframe covered with cedar panels (at the front) and Michelin rubberized fabric.

Wings Span 42ft (12.8m). Area 538 sq ft (50 sq m). The wing surface is in two parts connected by the main spars which are mounted on brackets attached to the body. The rear bracket is pivoted to allow the wings to be warped by the pilot. The wings are also supported by wires radiating from a wooden post projecting above the body.

The Antoinette monoplanes were probably the most elegant aircraft of the period and their appearance was enhanced by the elevator and rudder which were arranged like the feathers of an arrow. The various control movements were carried out by wheels on the sides of the cockpit.

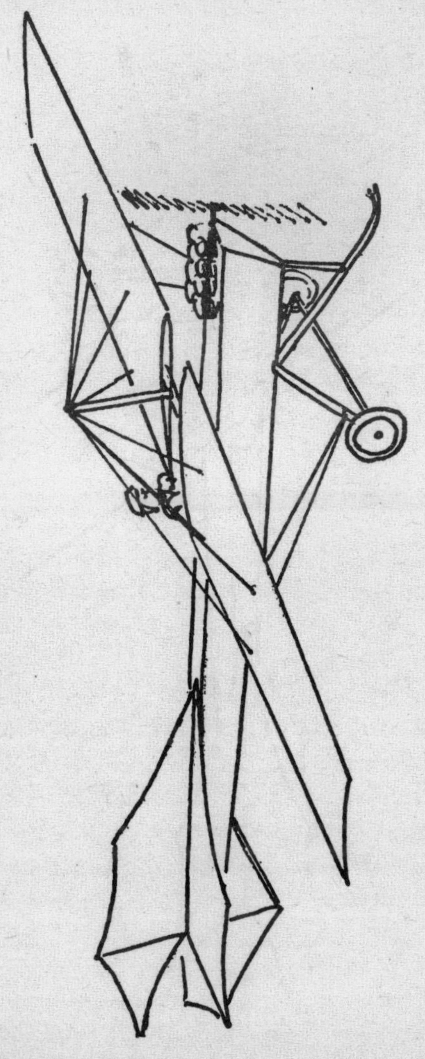

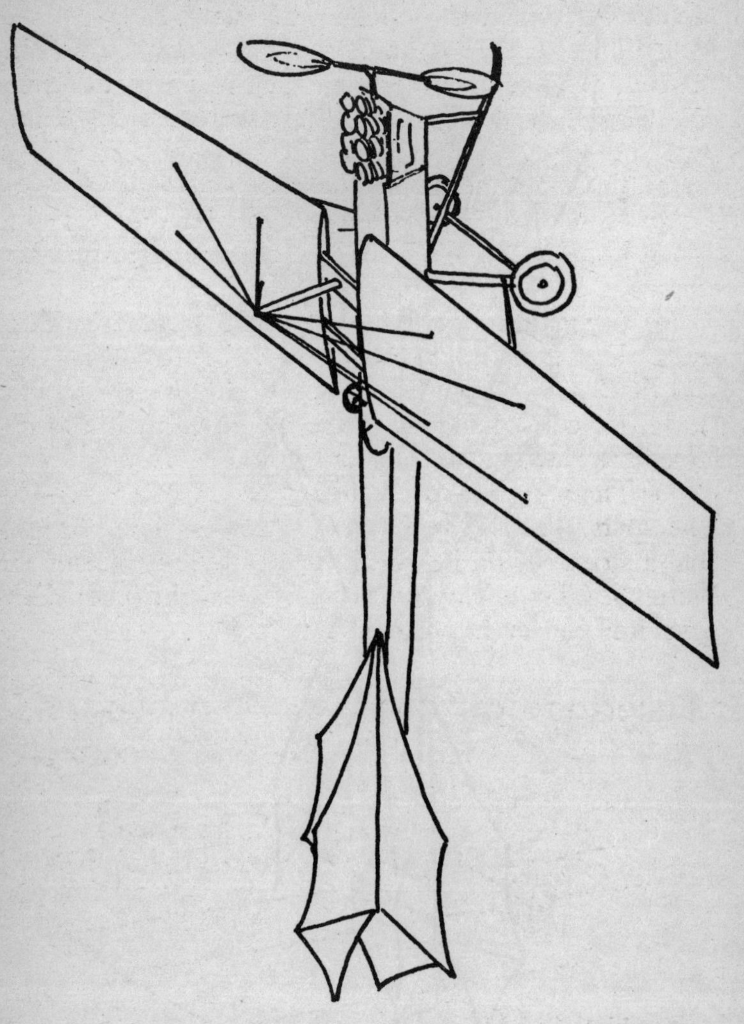

To Make the Antoinette VII

Follow the stages in the general instructions paying particular attention to the following details:

(1) The fuselage is made in two sections. The two halves are made separately and then joined by inserting the tabs in the back section into the rear of the front section.

(2) The tailplane should be cut from two thicknesses of card glued together before cutting to shape. It is then glued in place to the rear of the fuselage in the position shown.

(3) The main rudder is folded to give the double thickness, glued together and then stuck to the *tailplane and the fuselage top* and supported until the glue is dry. The lower rudder, again folded and glued, is stuck into the rear of the fuselage by the shaded tab.

(4) The wings are not joined in the middle except by the spars, $\frac{1}{4}$in × $\frac{1}{16}$in (6mm × 1.5mm) balsa. The two balsa strips should be glued to the lower surface of the wings leaving a gap $\frac{5}{8}$in (15mm) between them. Fold over and glue in the normal way.

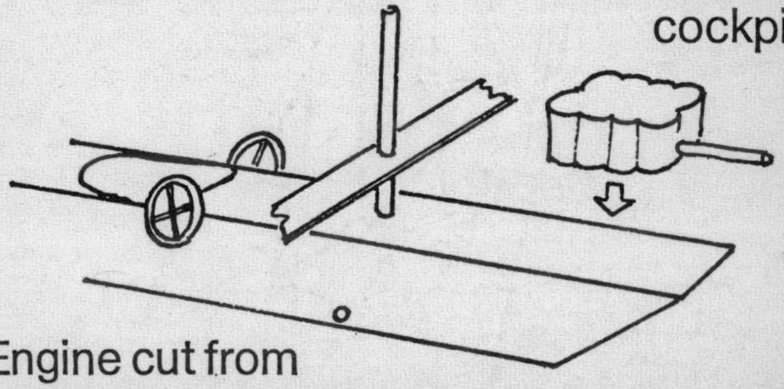

Fuselage top showing wing mounting and cockpit.

Engine cut from soft balsa with dowel for propeller shaft.

(5) The wings are attached to the fuselage by a cocktail stick or $\frac{1}{16}$in (1.5mm) dowel 2in (5cm) long. The dowel is glued into the fuselage and the hole in the middle of the front spar with the spar $\frac{5}{16}$in (8mm) above the fuselage. The top of the dowel serves as the rigging pylon.

(6) The undercarriage and skid details are shown in the diagram together with the bracing wire positions.

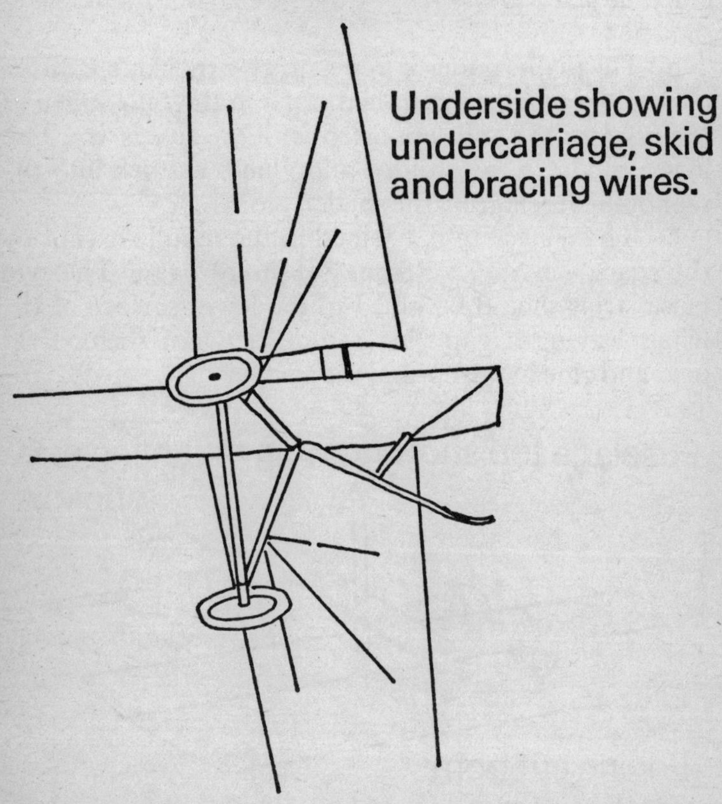

Underside showing undercarriage, skid and bracing wires.

Model Plans

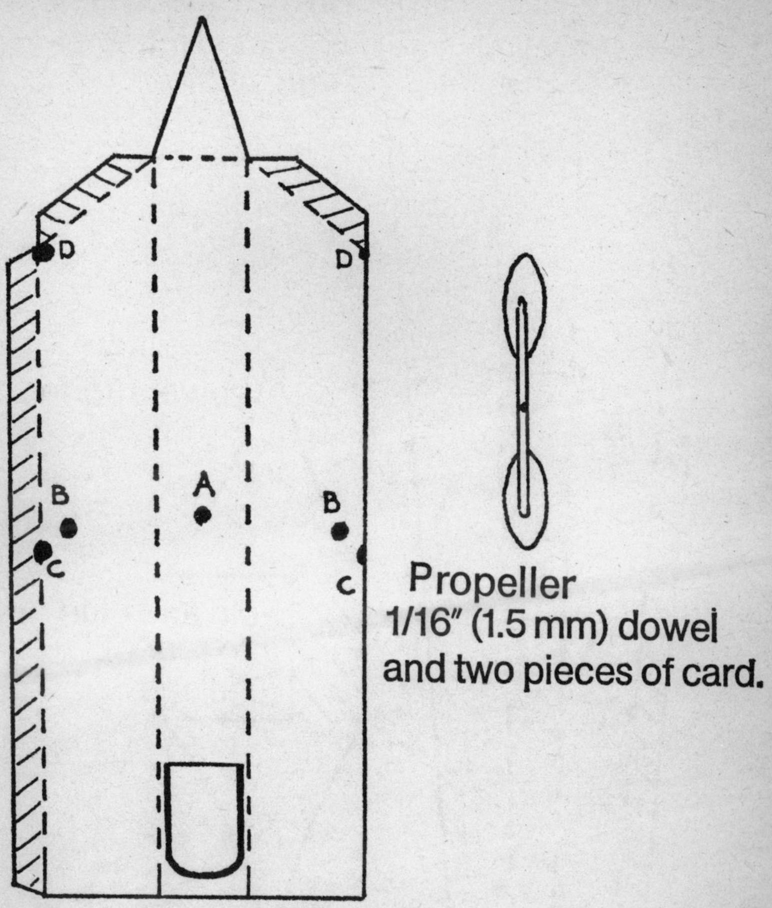

Propeller
1/16″ (1.5 mm) dowel
and two pieces of card.

Fuselage front section.

A. Hole for wing support dowel
B.B. Holes for undercarriage
C.D. Holes for skid

This section is painted brown. The rest of the model should be beige.

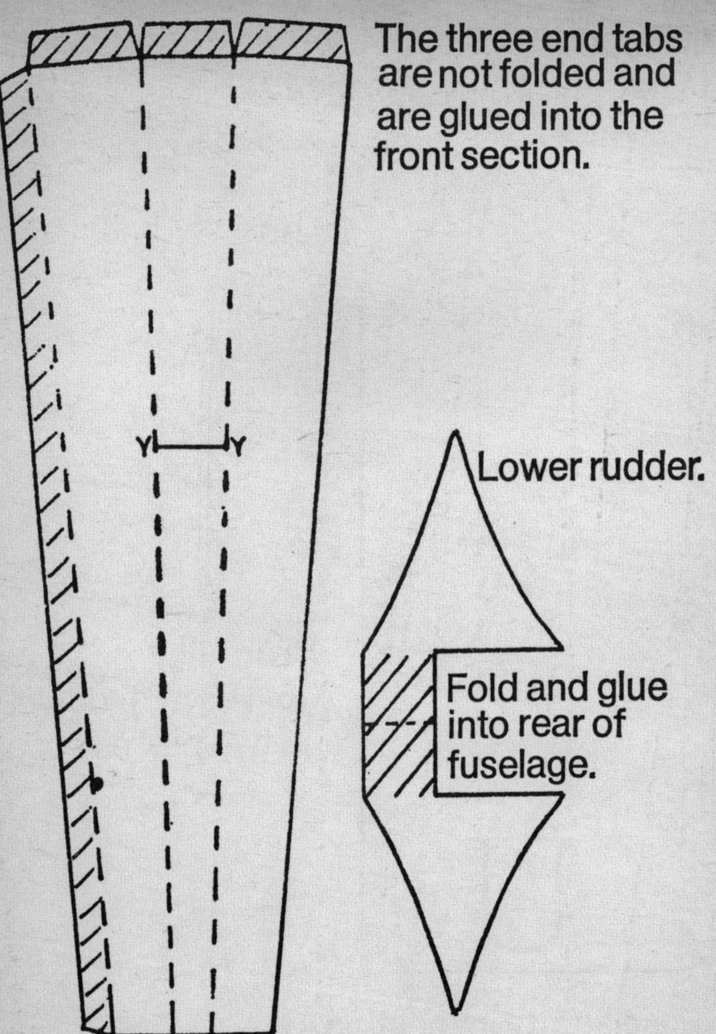

Fuselage rear section.

Line YY shows position of front edge of tailplane.

Balsa strips joining the two wings (leaving a ⅝″ (15 mm) gap between them).

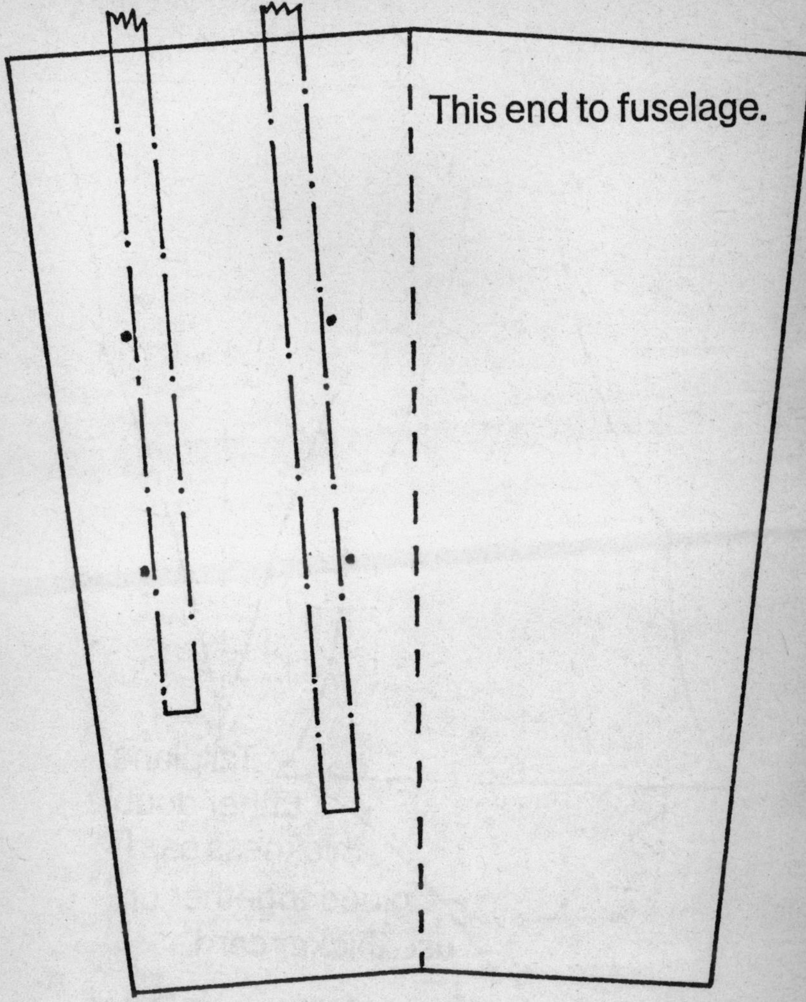

Main wing. *Two* required. Holes for bracing wire shown in lower surface only.

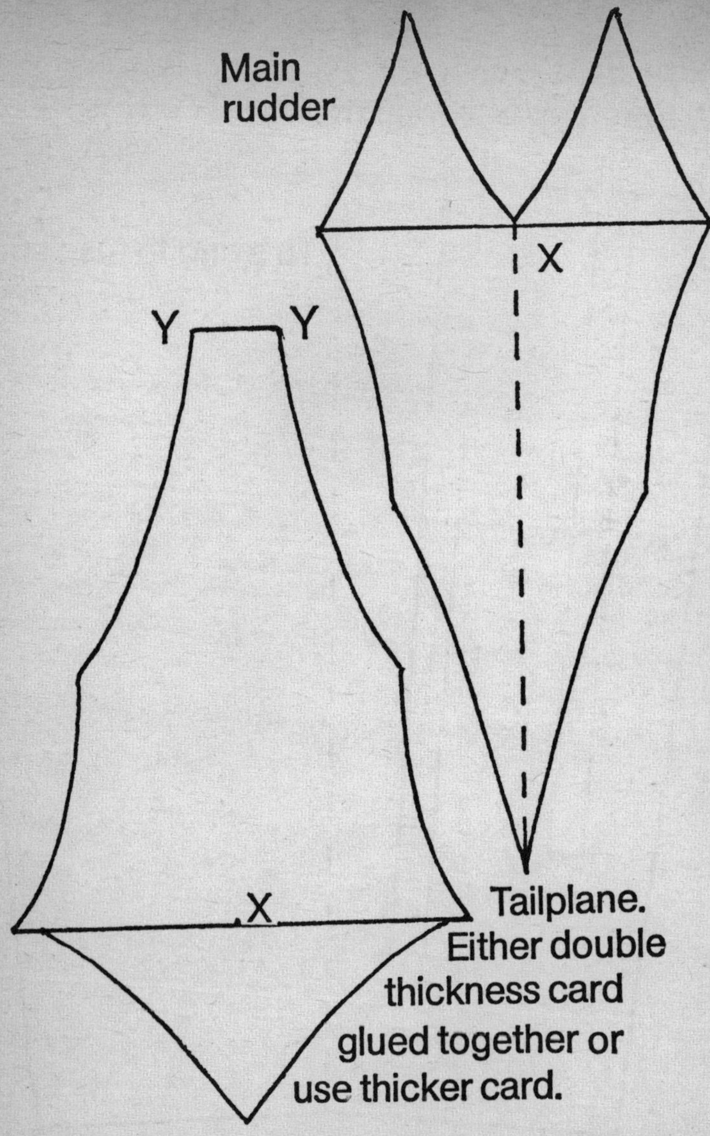

Main rudder is glued to tailplane. Point X on the rudder to point X on the tailplane.

Curtiss Flying Boat

In January 1907 Glenn Hammond Curtiss established the World Motor Cycle Speed Record of 136mph (219.35km/h) on a machine built in his workshops. Later that year he turned his attention to aviation and joined the American Aerial Experimentation Associa-ation. His main contributions to the work of the AEA were his Vee-type engines but he slowly emerged as a designer being mainly responsible for the third aeroplane built by the Association and known as the *June Bug*. On the 4th July, 1908, this plane won a prize for the first officially recorded flight in America of more than 1km. This prize should have been won by the Wright Brothers but their flights were not officially recognized.

Curtiss then left the Association and joined Augustus N. Herring in forming the first Aircraft manufacturing company in the United States. They produced a biplane in the Spring of 1909 which was so successful that a more powerful version was started almost immediately. This plane made its maiden flight at the Grande Semaine d'Aviation de la Champagne Rheims, France, on the 25th August, 1909, and during the next four days Curtiss won two major races.

With this plane, the *Golden Flyer*, Curtiss made some very important contributions to aviation. In June 1910 he demonstrated a mock bombing attack on a dummy warship. In August the first air-to-ground wireless message was sent from a Curtiss machine and in November a *Golden Flyer* took off from a platform aboard a ship. In January 1911 another Curtiss plane landed on a similar platform aboard the U.S.S. Pennsylvania in San Francisco Bay. These events marked the birth of the aircraft carrier, and the arrester cables and hooks used then were much the same as we know them today.

Curtiss had impressed the U.S. Army and Navy and several of his machines were bought by them. A lot of experiments were conducted with floats fitted to aircraft, and Curtiss concentrated his attention on seaplanes. In January 1912 the *Curtiss Flying Boat* made its first flight. This was a new development in waterborne aircraft having a boat-shaped hull and, after several modifications, was adopted by the U.S. Navy. It was an excellent machine and later that year one became the first aeroplane to fly with a gyroscopic automatic pilot.

Curtiss Flying Boat 1914 U.S.A.

Power One 100hp Curtiss water-cooled V8 engine mounted between the wings driving a laminated mahogany 'pusher' propeller.
Wings Span: 39ft (11.9m) upper; 28ft (8.5m) lower, covered in bleached linen.
Fuselage 27ft 4in long cross lapped mahogany strips on spruce and pine frame. The shape of the hull was based on current speed boat design and could carry a passenger sitting beside the pilot in the wide cockpit.

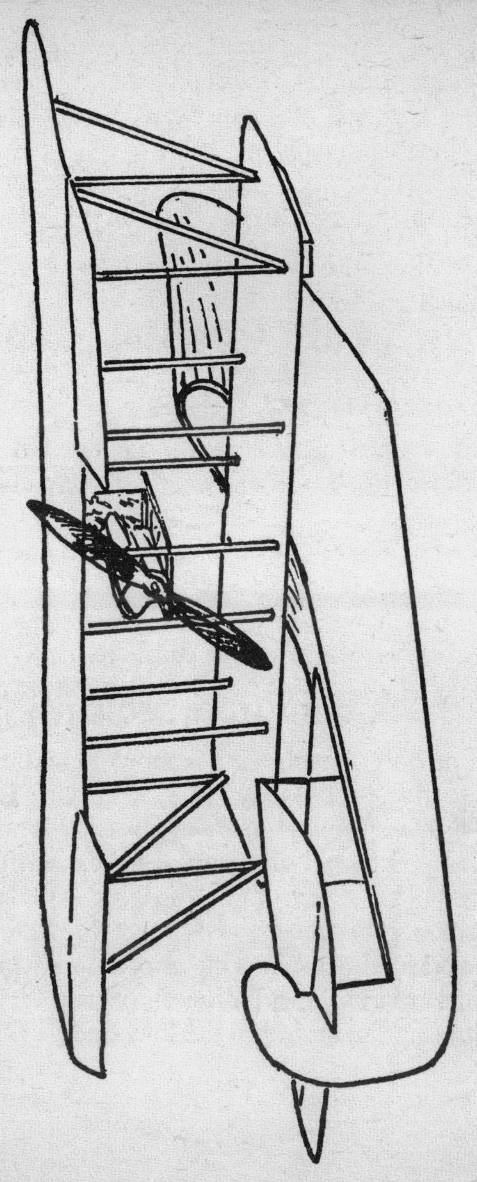

To Make the Curtiss Flying Boat

The fuselage of this model may appear complicated but should present no difficulty if prepared carefully.

(1) Cut out the two main sections and assemble the rear part in the normal way.

(2) Cut out and glue in place the fuselage front bottom. The top decking can now be glued in place.

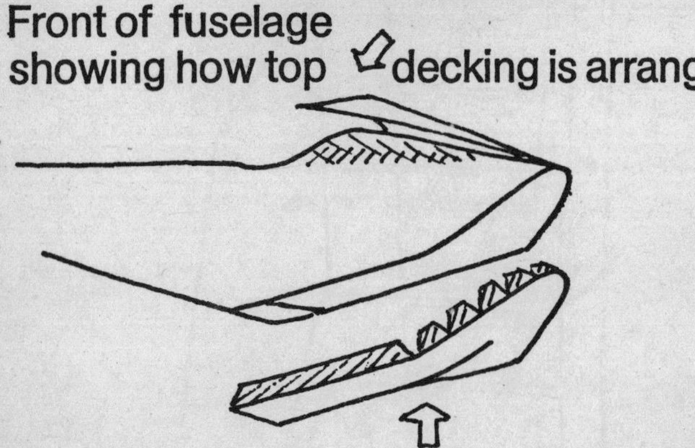

(3) Only one half of each wing is shown. Cut out a pair and complete in the usual way. The lower wing is mounted on the flat section behind the cockpit. The upper wing is supported by 16 pieces of $\frac{1}{16}$in (1.5mm) dowel. Cut 12 pieces $1\frac{1}{4}$in (3.2cm) long and glue into the holes in the top surface of the lower wing. Glue the tops of these struts and fix the upper wing in position. Make sure that the wings are in line and allow the glue to dry. Cut 4 lengths $1\frac{1}{16}$in (4.3cm) and trim the lower edge. Glue into place.

(4) The rudder is prepared and glued in position. The tabs are folded outwards and the tailplane is glued to them. The front end of the tailplane is supported by a short length of dowel.

Details of rudder and elevator construction.

(5) Make two floats and fix under the ends of the lower wing.

(6) Cut out and assemble the engine, glue between the centre wing struts and fit the propeller if you wish.

(7) Finish the model with the bracing wires and paint the hull dark brown (mahogany) and the wings beige.

Model Plans

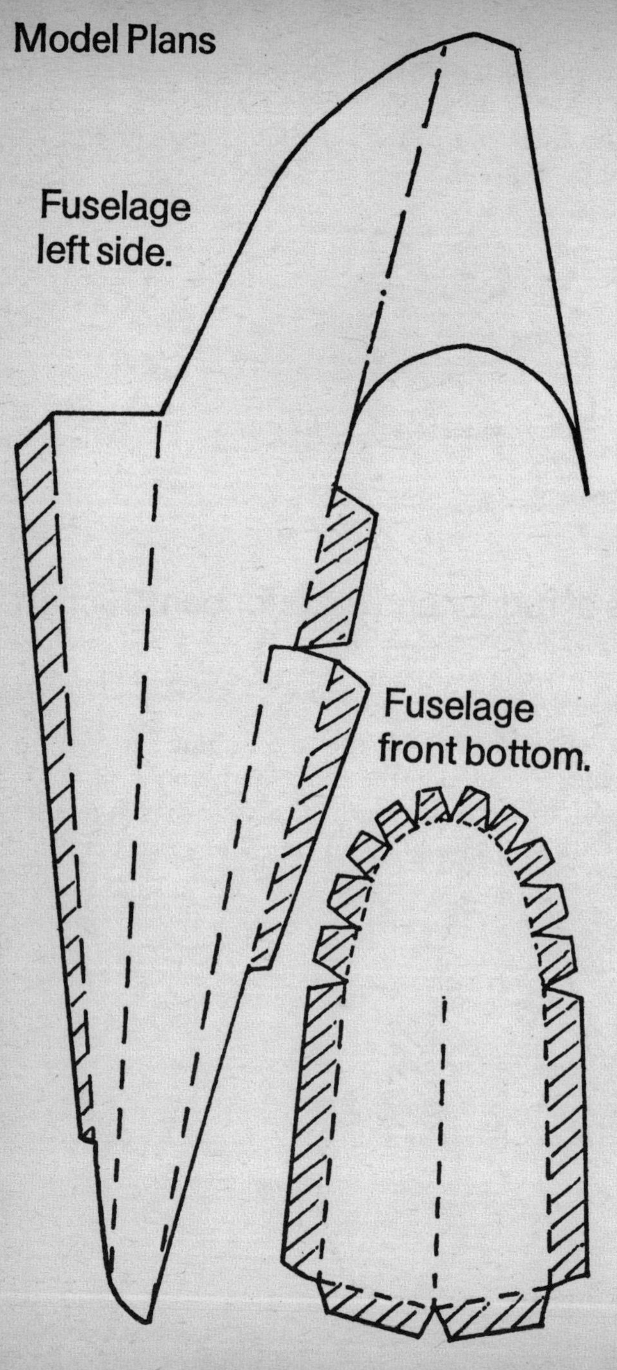

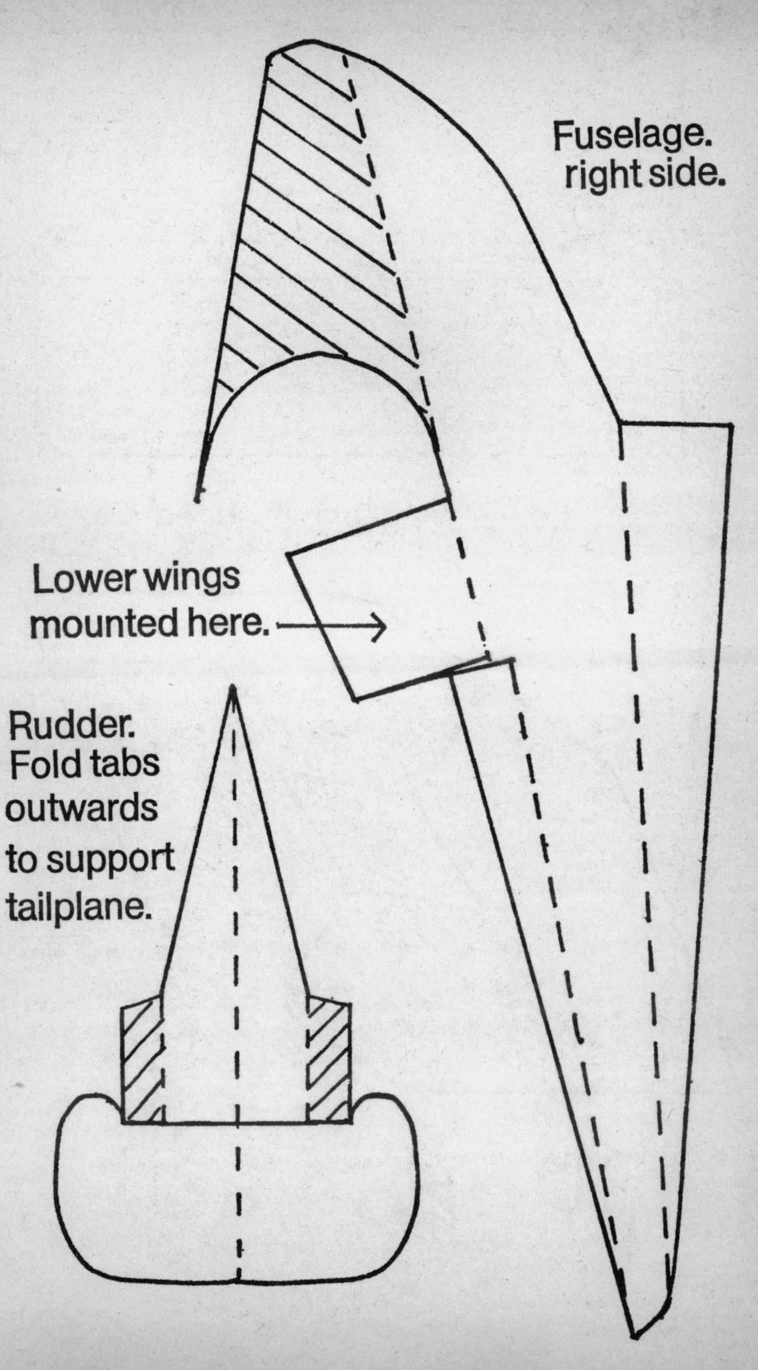
Fuselage.
right side.
Lower wings
mounted here.
Rudder.
Fold tabs
outwards
to support
tailplane.

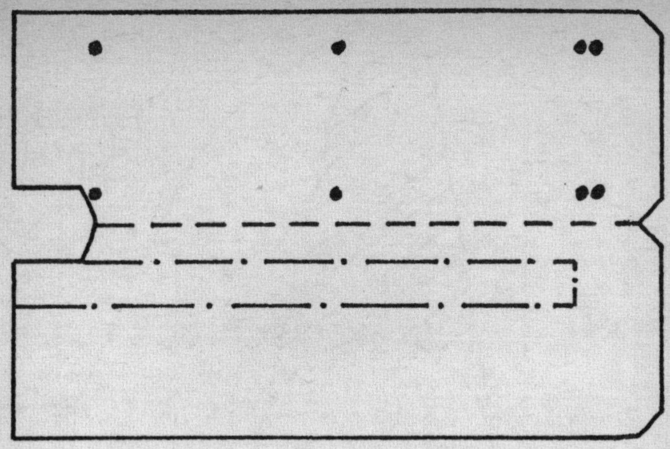

Lower wing. Two required.

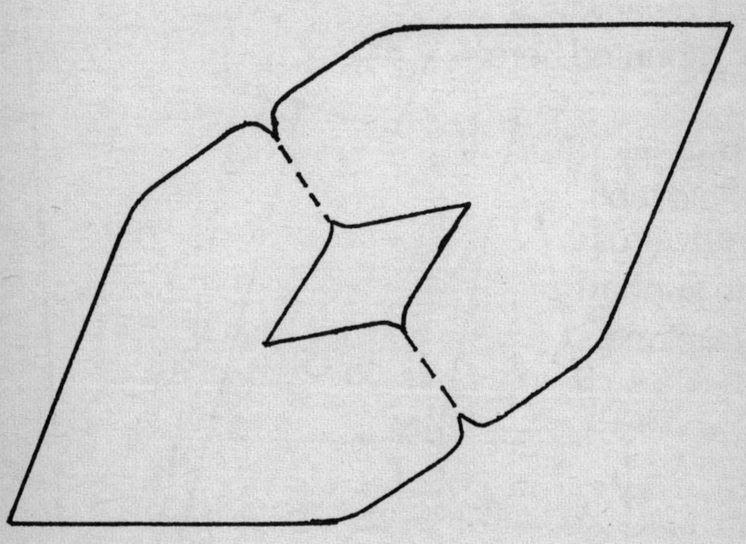

Tailplane.

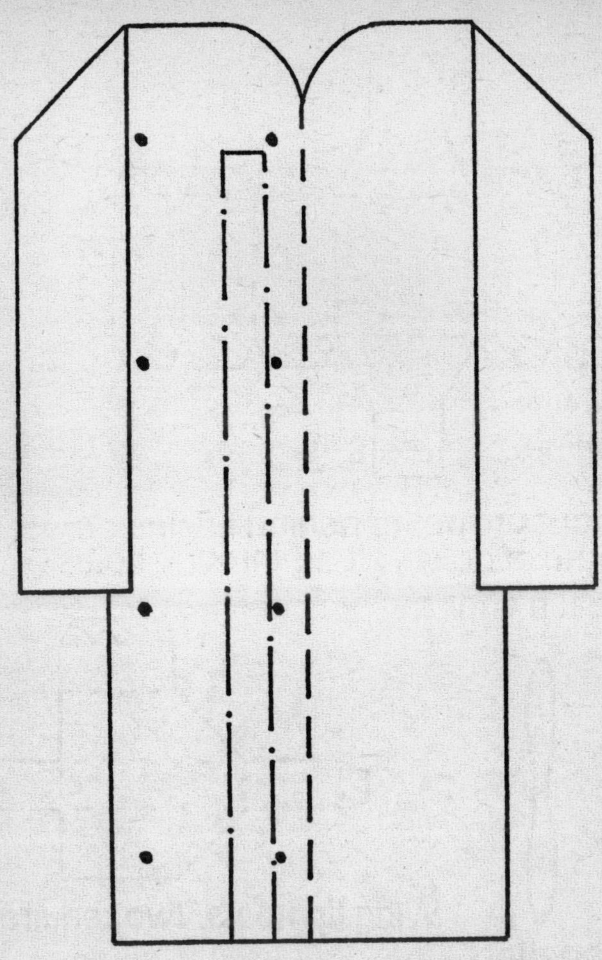

Upper wing. Two required.

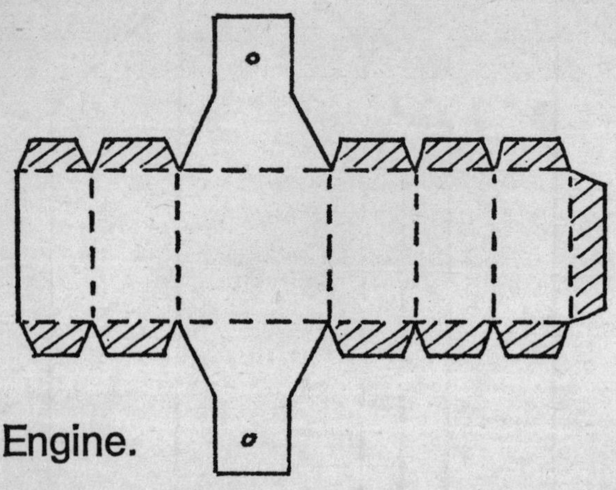

Engine.

Mount propeller behind engine on length of dowel glued through holes in each end.

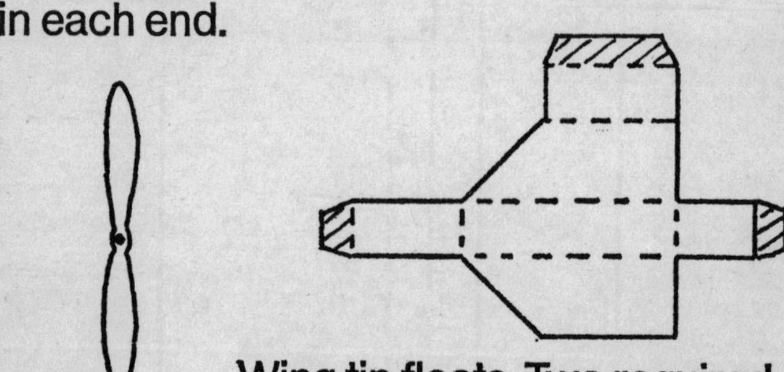

Wing tip floats. Two required.

Propeller
Cut from card or balsa.

xx **BE 2a**

Geoffrey de Havilland was one of the most famous of the British Aviation Pioneers. He was the son of a clergyman but interested only in engineering from boyhood and built his first aeroplane, with his friend, Frank Hearle, in 1908 when he was 25 years old. The plane crashed on its first attempt to take off and was damaged beyond repair. A second machine was built, using the salvaged engine, and this one flew very well. De Havilland, D.H., as he was known, was one of the few pioneers who built not only his aeroplane but also its engine and then learned to fly on it.

D.H. had almost run out of money by now but his experiments had impressed the Government who offered him and Hearle jobs at the Royal Aircraft Factory at Farnborough in 1910 and bought his plane for £400. The factory was intended for the repair and reconstruction and not the building of aircraft but the staff interpreted reconstruction very freely and in fact designed new machines incorporating some parts, particularly the engines, of those they were to repair.

On January 1st, 1912, de Havilland made the first flight in a 'new' biplane, known as the *BE*. This first flight proved so promising that a programme of experimental work was set up to develop the design and led to a series of *BE's* which were to become one of the mainstays of Britain's air effort in the early stages of the First World War.

Farnborough supplied a variety of aircraft for service during the war and all were known by numbers rather than names. Included among these were the *FE 2b*, the *RE 8* and, perhaps the best known of all was the *SE 5a*.

After the war de Havilland formed his own company and became one of Britain's major aircraft manufacturers. A very popular small plane made by the company was the *Tiger Moth* biplane. During the Second World War the R.A.F. used several de Havilland aircraft including the *Mosquito* which was unusual in that it was built almost completely in wood. After the war the company led the World by putting into service the first jet engined airliner, the *Comet*.

BE 2a 1913 Reconnaissance Biplane

Power One 70hp Renault 8-cylinder Vee-type air-cooled engine driving a 4-bladed mahogany propeller 9ft (2.65m) diameter.
Fuselage Ash and spruce frame, 29ft 6in (9.00m) long, covered with aluminium, plywood and linen.
Wings Span 35ft (10.68m). Area 352 sq ft (32.7 sq m), built of wood and aluminium covered with unbleached linen.

The aeroplane had a wheeled undercarriage and two skids to protect the propeller. It also had a rear skid which moved with the rudder to allow the machine to be steered on land.

Just over 5 years after Bleriot's historic flight another Channel crossing was made, this time three squadrons of the Royal Flying Corps flew from Dover to France. The date was 13th August, 1914. It was the first war time mass flight across national boundaries in history and the first plane to cross was a *BE 2a* of No. 2 Squadron.

347

To Make the BE 2a

(1) The fuselage is constructed in the usual way. Note the long vee tab at the front, this is used to eliminate the taper.

(2) The cockpits/engine cowl is cut out and scored as shown and then rounded before fitting in position. It is then glued along the inside edge and fitted to the top of the fuselage sides.

The front end is tapered by the Vee tab. Front of model showing fitting of cockpits/engine cowl.

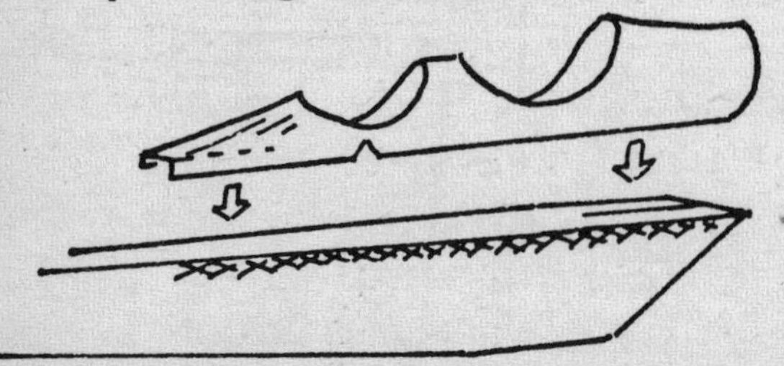

(3) Both halves of the lower wing are shown, prepare them in the usual way with a balsa strip in each and then mount under the fuselage. The top wing is now made, cut out two halves and assemble with one balsa strip. This wing is mounted directly above the lower one, cut out eight $1\frac{1}{2}$in (3.8cm) lengths of $\frac{1}{16}$in (1.5mm) dowel and glue into the eight holes in the top surface of the lower wing. Glue the top wing on to these struts, check for squareness and leave to dry.

(4) Prepare the tailplane and glue to the top of the fuselage and then make up the rudder and glue into the rear by the shaded tab.

(5) Make the undercarriage from $\frac{1}{16}$in (1.5mm) dowel as shown in the diagram. The wheels, cut from thicker card, are $\frac{5}{8}$in (1.7mm) diameter.

(6) Finish the model with bracing wires and propeller if you wish and paint it beige with the engine cowl aluminium.

Undercarriage.

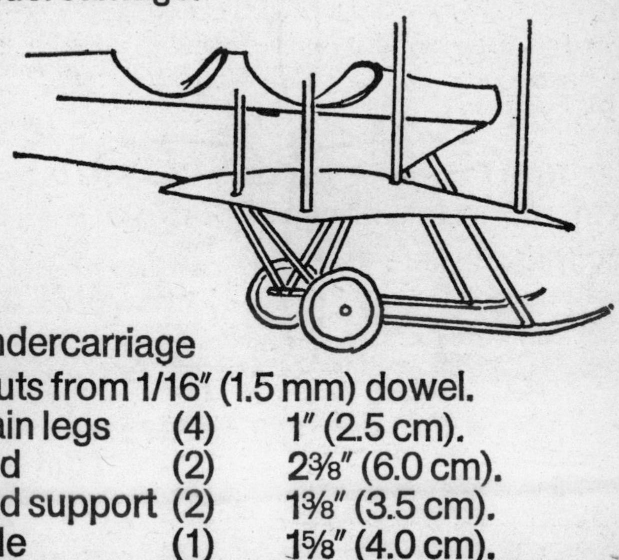

Undercarriage
struts from 1/16″ (1.5 mm) dowel.

Main legs	(4)	1″ (2.5 cm).
Skid	(2)	2⅜″ (6.0 cm).
Skid support	(2)	1⅜″ (3.5 cm).
Axle	(1)	1⅝″ (4.0 cm).

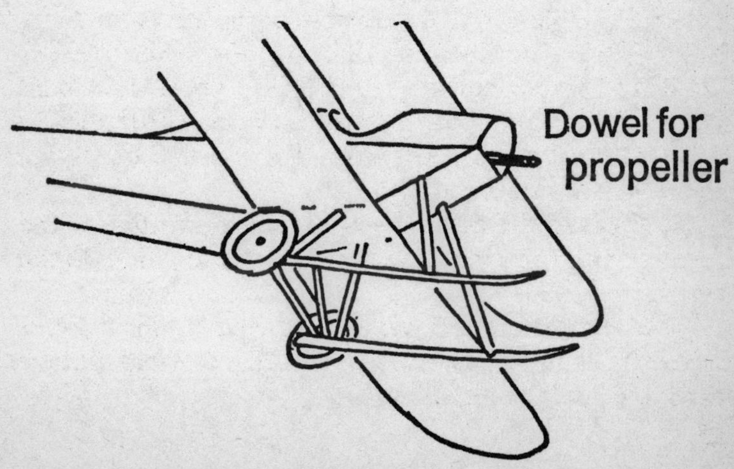

Propeller, cut from thick card is on short length of dowel glued into nose of model.

Model Plans

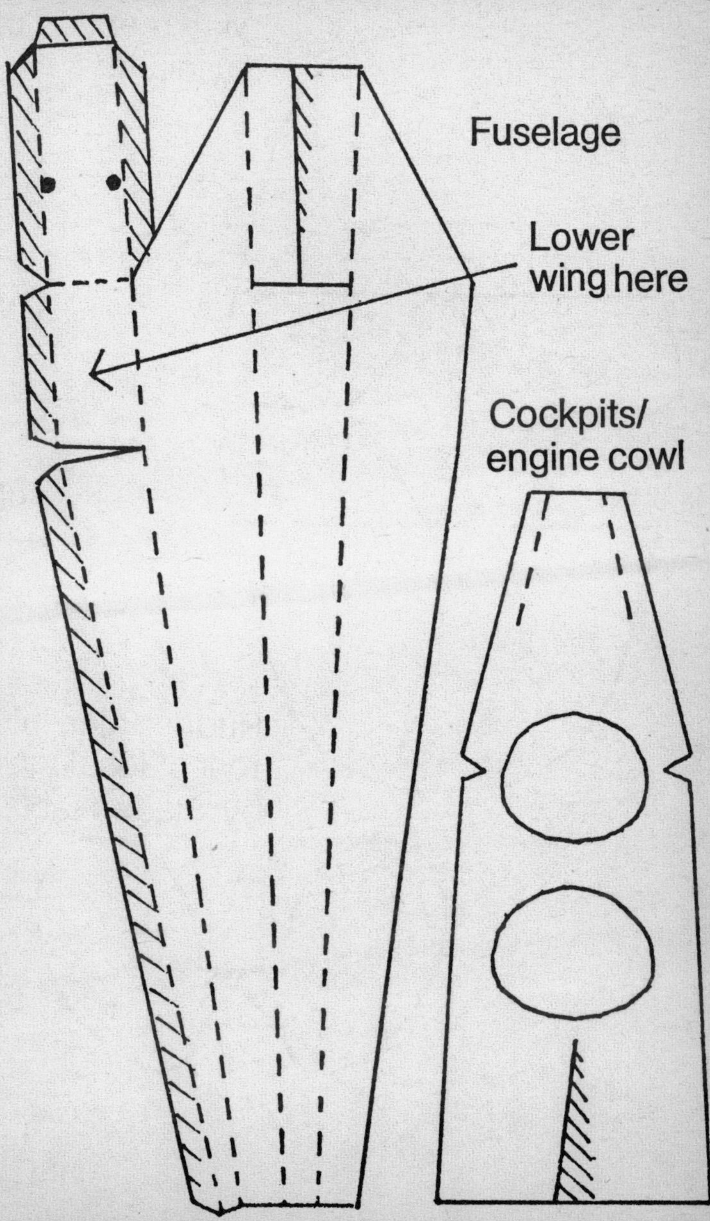

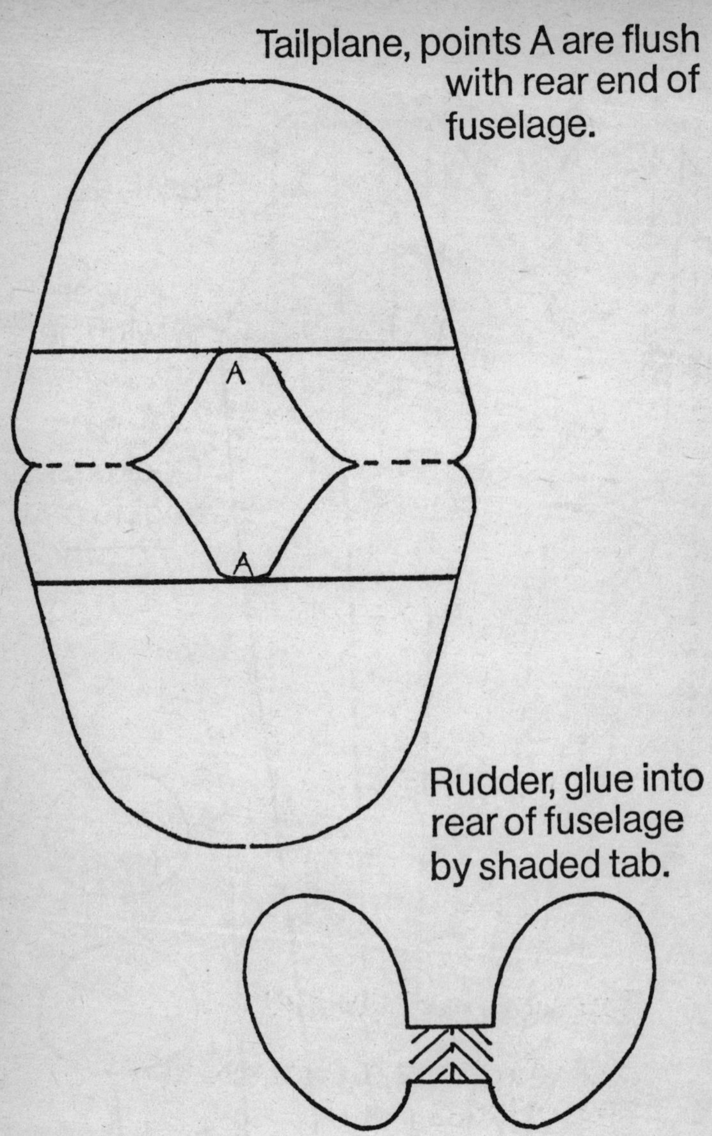

Tailplane, points A are flush with rear end of fuselage.

Rudder, glue into rear of fuselage by shaded tab.

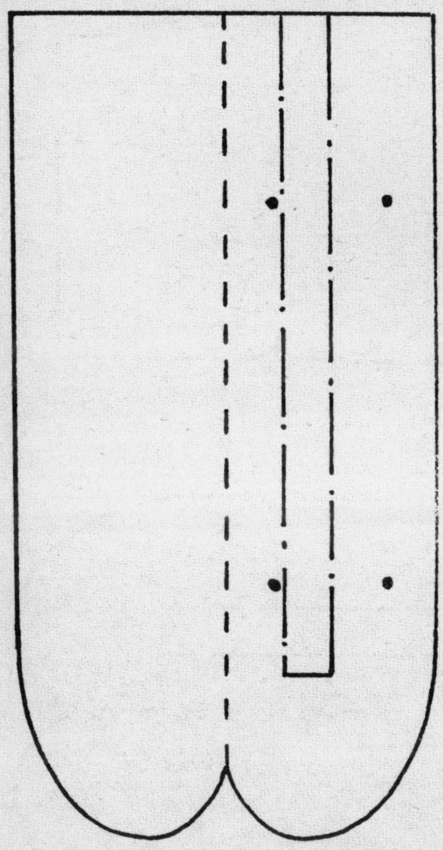

Top wing. Two required.

Join with piece of card and long strip of balsa.

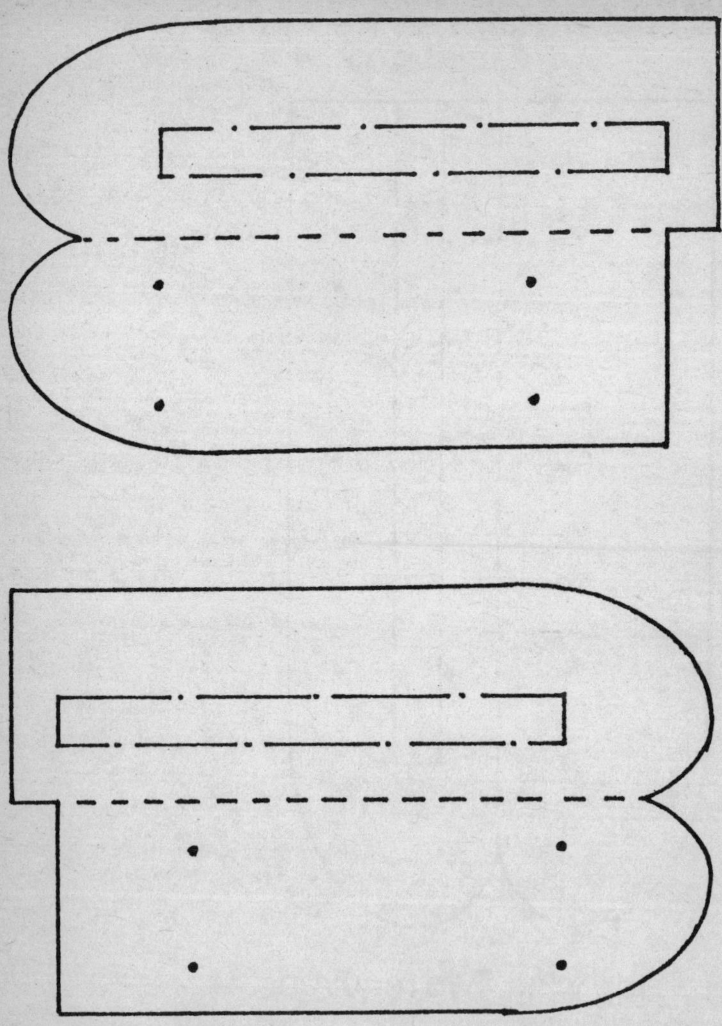

Lower wings. Make up separately and glue below the fuselage and to the sides.

xx **Nieuport Scout**

Nieuport is perhaps one of the greatest names of the pioneer years of flying. Edouard de Niéport was born in France in 1875 and became an engineer. He was also a keen sportsman. In 1909 he formed a company – the Société Anonyme des Etablissements Nieuport – to build aeroplanes. The company soon established an international reputation as a producer of several very good fast monoplanes.

Early Nieuport planes were very successful in races and in record breaking. In May 1911 a *Type II N* set up a world speed record of 74.37mph (119.68km/hr). A *Type IV G* won the French military prize in November of that year. A Nieuport also won the Gordon Bennett Trophy for 1911 and one set up a distance record of 460 miles (740.255km). In 1913 a Nieuport set a new world altitude records at over 20,000ft (6.120m) and a Russian pilot became the first man ever to loop the loop, in a Nieuport.

Nieuport monoplanes were sold to the Italian, Russian and British air forces in the years before WW I. In January 1914 an engineer named Gustave Delage became Chief Designer and put into production the first biplane built by the company. This plane set the pattern for a series of military aircraft which were used not only by the French but by the Belgians, the Italians, the British and the American forces. The design was in fact so successful the Germans copied a captured *Nieuport 17* in their *Siemens–Schuckert D I.*

The biplane, designed by Delage, was of unusual layout. The lower wing was much smaller than the upper one which gave the pilot much of the speed and manoeuvrability of a monoplane with the strength and other benefits of a biplane. The narrow lower wing also gave the pilot much better visibility than that of the conventional biplane. This one-and-a-half wing design was used on all Nieuport models until the beginning of 1918 and the appearance of the *Type 28*.

The *Type 17* was, perhaps, the most famous of the family and many wartime aces flew it at some time. The Frenchmen Charles Nungesser and Georges Guynemer, Albert Ball from Britain and the Canadian, William Avery Bishop, scored many victories with this plane.

Nieuport Type 17 Fighting Scout 1916 France

Power Either 110hp Le Rhône or 130hp Clerget Rotary engine driving a two-bladed wooden propeller 8ft (2.44m) diameter.
Fuselage Braced wooden box girder with steel strengtheners covered in aluminium and fabric. 19ft 7in (5.97m) long.
Wings Span: Top wing 26ft (7.93m); Lower wing 25ft 7in (7.80m).

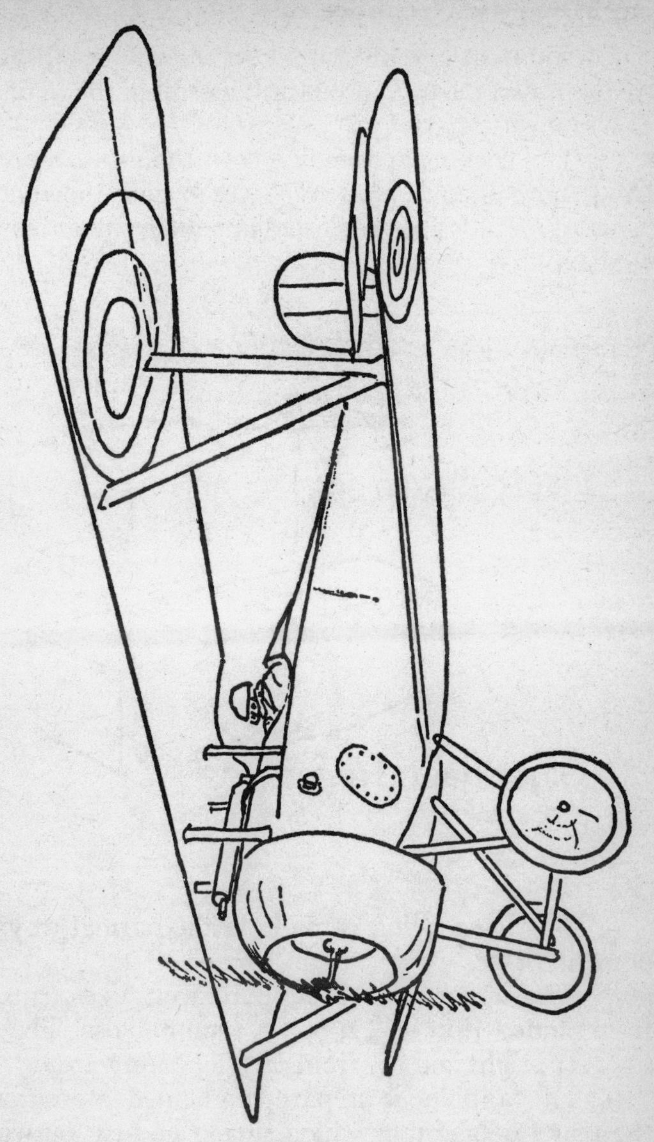

To Make the Nieuport 17

(1) The fuselage of this model is quite small and is made in two parts. Cut out and assemble the main section in the normal way.

(2) The cockpit and engine cowl should be scored as shown and then curved to shape to give the rounded nose. A soft balsa block is fitted into the front and sanded to shape.

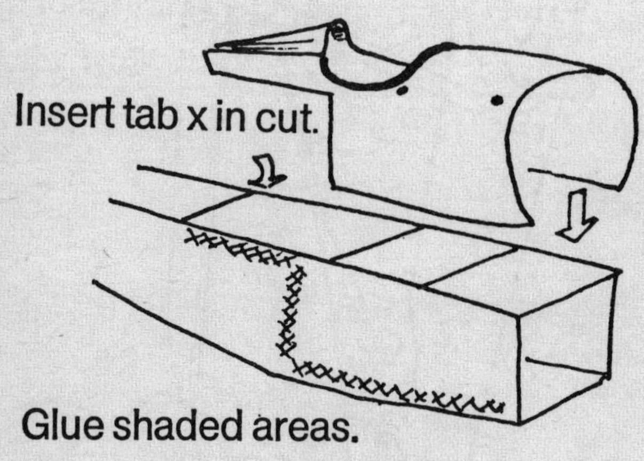

(3) The lower wing is made in the normal way and glued in place.

(4) The upper wing is supported on Vee struts cut from sanded $\frac{3}{16}$in × $\frac{1}{16}$in (4.5 × 1.5mm) balsa. The rear strut is upright and the front one slopes forward.

(5) The tailplane is prepared and glued in position on the rear fuselage tabs which should be bent outwards. The rudder can now be glued in position.

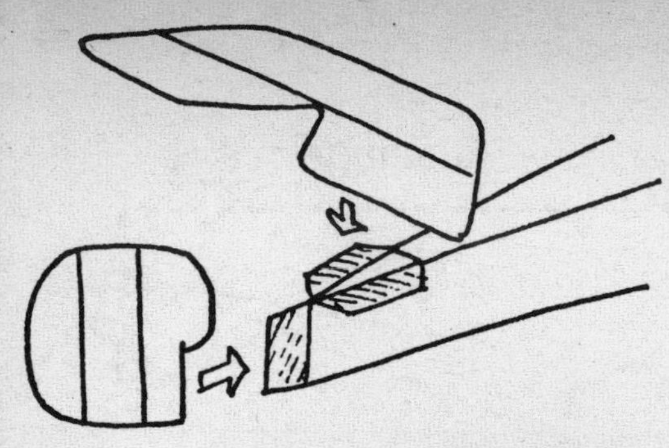

Rear of fuselage showing tailplane and rudder fixing. Rudder halves are glued either side of fuselage end tab.

Undercarriage struts 1¼″ (3.2 cm) long. Axle 1⅜″ (3.5 cm) long.

(6) The undercarriage is made from $\frac{1}{16}$in (1.5mm) dowel and the wheels are cut from thick card $\frac{9}{16}$in (1.4cm) diameter.

(7) Complete the model with the bracing wires and propeller if you wish and paint it silver grey.

Propeller.
Cut from stiff card or balsa.

Model Plans

Lower wing here.
Fuselage.
A
A
Points AA:
Undercarriage
front struts.
X
X
X
X
Cockpit/engine cowl.
Cut line xx on fuselage to
take tabs xx on cockpit.
Tailplane.

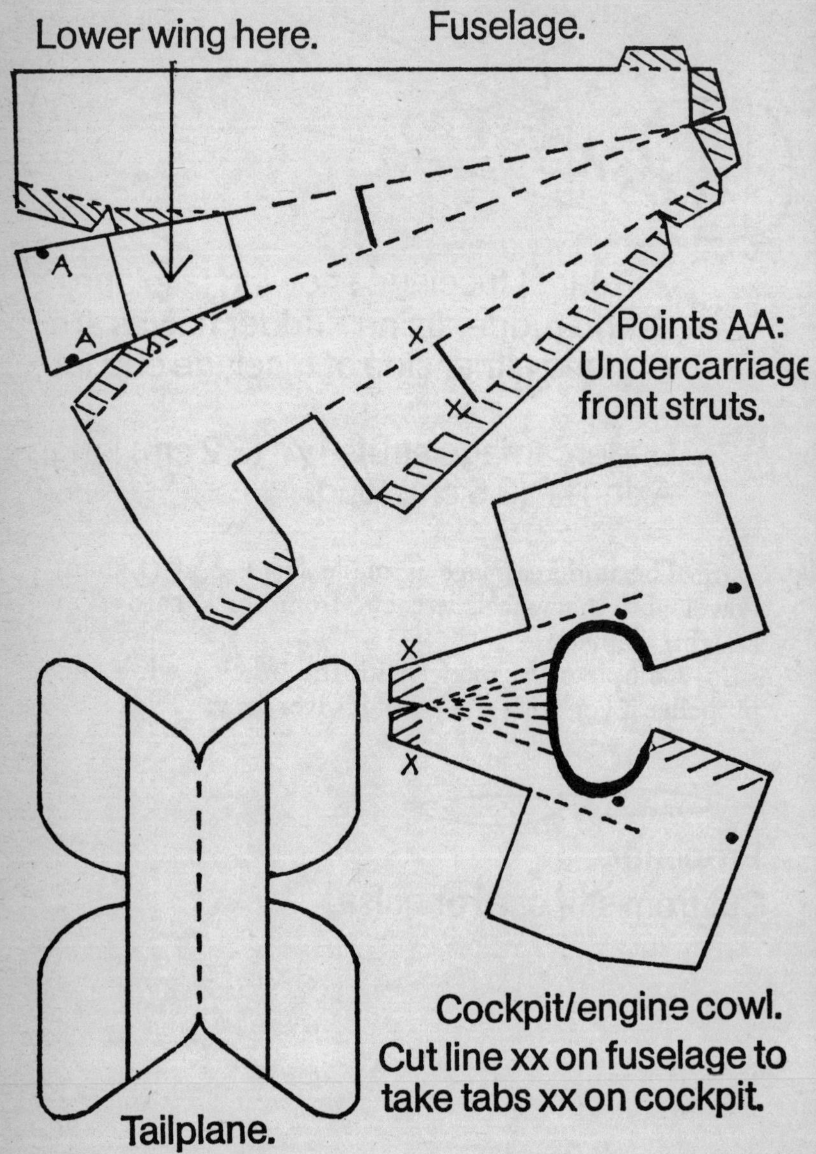

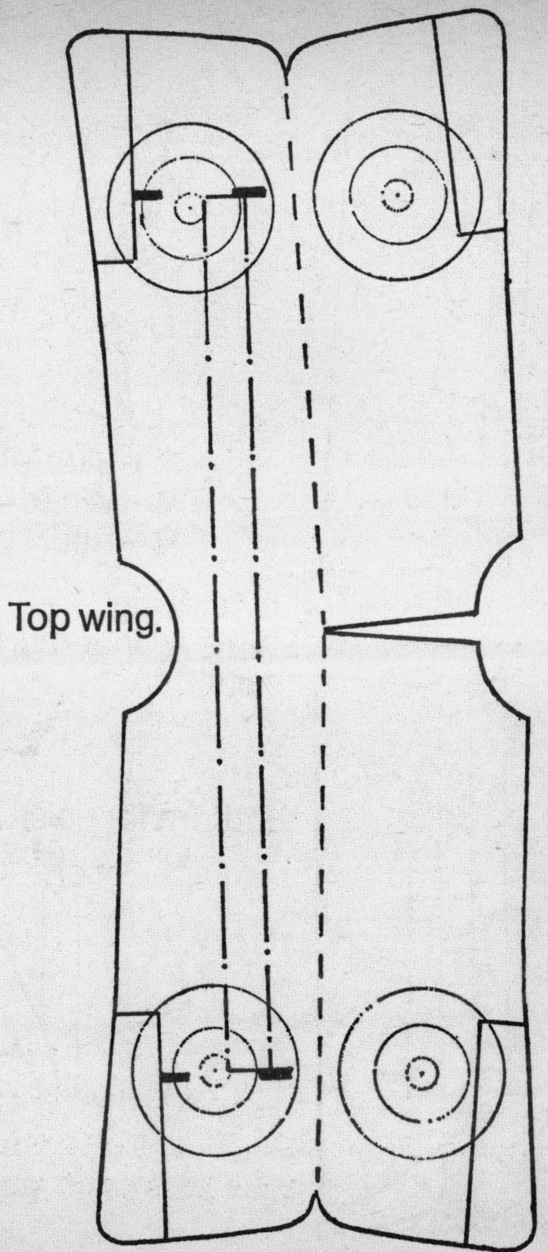
Top wing.

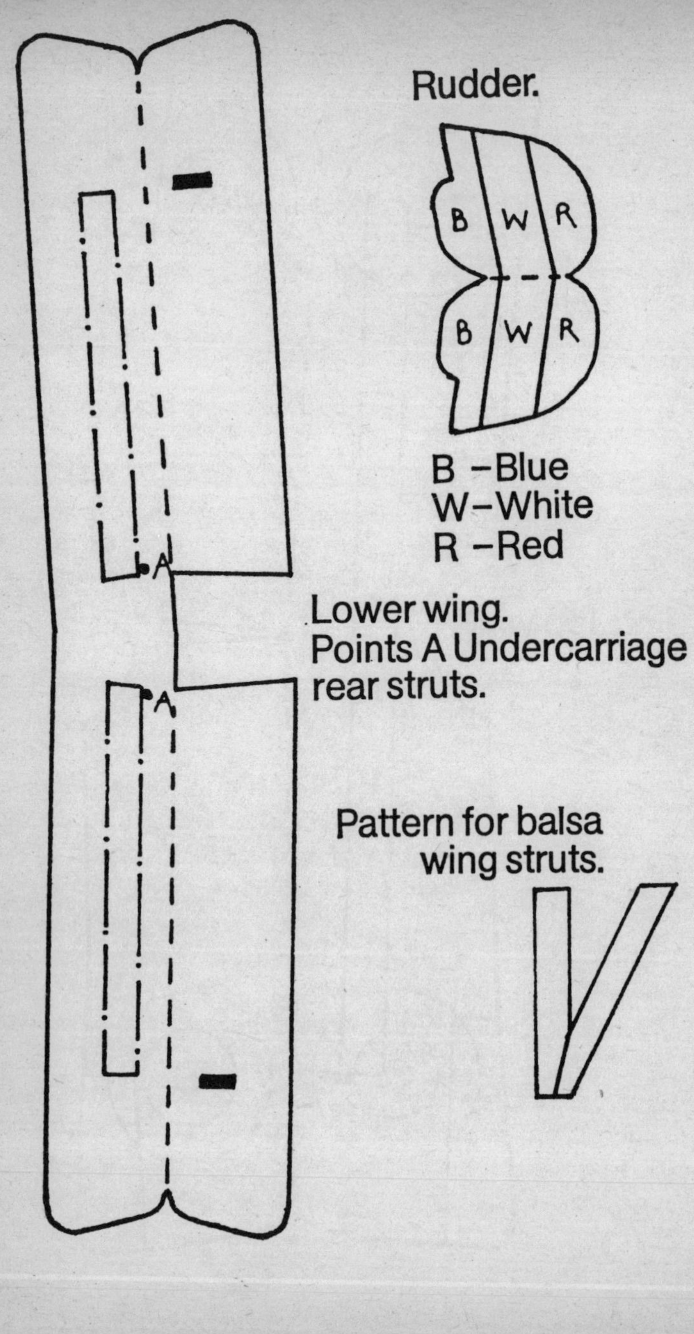
Rudder.
B
W
R
B
W
R
B –Blue
W–White
R –Red
A
A
Lower wing.
Points A Undercarriage
rear struts.
Pattern for balsa
wing struts.

Fokker

In 1908 when Wilbur Wright demonstrated his aeroplane in France, an eighteen-year-old Dutch student became very interested in flying. Two years later, having finished his studies and completed his national service, Anthony Herman Gerard Fokker built his first aeroplane. Fokker did not have any special technical knowledge or training but he was a natural pilot with a 'feel' for what was good design. This aeroplane was built in Germany in partnership with Franz von Daum, who, in Fokker's absence, attempted his first flight and wrote-off the plane by taxiing it into a tree.

A second machine was built and again Von Daum crashed it and Fokker broke up the partnership. Fokker then built his third aeroplane, smaller than the first two and capable of carrying a passenger. It flew in August 1911 and earned the nickname *Haarlem Spin* (*Spider*). About 25 Spins were built at Fokker's factory near Berlin and were either sold to private fliers or used by the Fokker Flying School.

The aircraft was tested by the Prussian Army and led to a series of very important aircraft which were to play a major part in Germany's war effort. These pre-war military planes were not very popular with the pilots and their performance was not very good. Fokker realized in 1913 that he needed a new design if his firm was to survive. Fokker dismissed his designer and then produced a new monoplane, the *M5*, which was very similar to the French Morane-Saulnier in appearance but quite different in construction. After several modifications and improvements the new aircraft was very successful and was the mainstay of the German Imperial Air Service in the early part of the war.

These planes were known as *Eindeckers* and, of the 425 built, 260 were *EIII*'s. They were among the first fighter planes to be fitted with a synchronized machine-gun which fired bullets through the blades of the propeller by means of an interrupter mechanism. They were so accurate that they very nearly shot the Allied air forces from the skies over France in 1915 and early 1916.

By the summer of 1916 the new fighters of Britain and France were able to destroy the Fokker menace for a short time but by the end of the year the Germans regained their former air supremacy with a new breed of fighting machines.

About a year later the Fokker Company brought out a triplane, the *Dr I*, which, though rather slow, had a very good rate of climb and exceptional manoeuvrability. It was ideally suited to such pilots as Werner Voss who shot down 48 allied planes before he was killed in September 1917, and the legendary Baron Manfred von Richthofen who was credited with 80 killed, wounded or captured before he too was shot down and died on 21st April, 1918.

After the war Fokker returned to Holland and established a new company which produced many planes and played a big part in the development of civil aviation. Fokker transport planes were either used or copied by airlines all over the world and when he died in 1939 Anthony Fokker controlled a large and very successful business.

Fokker EIII 'Eindecker' **Germany 1915**

Power One 100hp Oberursel nine-cylinder rotary engine driving an 8ft 2in (2.50m) diameter 2-bladed propeller.

Fuselage Welded steel tube frame 24ft (7.30m) long covered with fabric with one, or sometimes two, Parabellum LMG 08 machine guns mounted in front of the cockpit.

Wings Fabric-covered wooden frame 31ft 3in (9.52m) span. Area 172 sq ft (160 sq m).

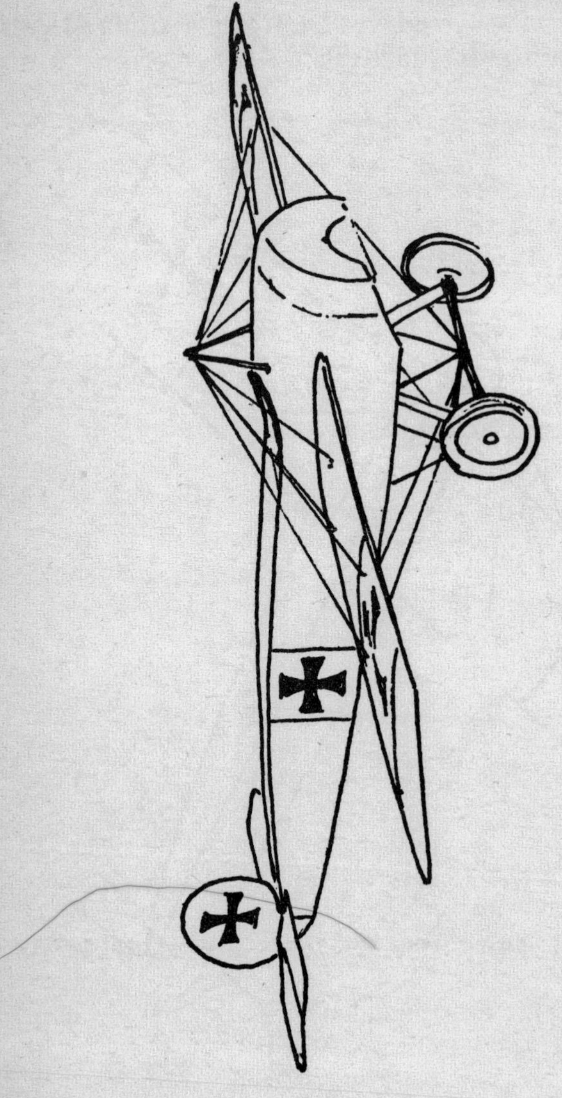

To Make the Fokker EIII

Follow the stages in the general instructions paying particular attention to the following details:

(1) Mark, score and cut out in the usual way. Cut out the cockpit and wing, fixing slots carefully, and assemble the fuselage.

(2) The wings are shown in two parts and should be joined before the balsa strip is fitted.

(3) Mark the bracing wire positions, there are four on each side.

(4) Assemble the wing and fit into the fuselage.

(5) The engine cowling is made by sticking a trimmed 'Smarties' lid, or a piece of $\frac{3}{16}$in (4.5mm) balsa $\frac{13}{16}$in (21mm) diameter cut as shown, to the front of the fuselage. The card cowl section is then glued in position.

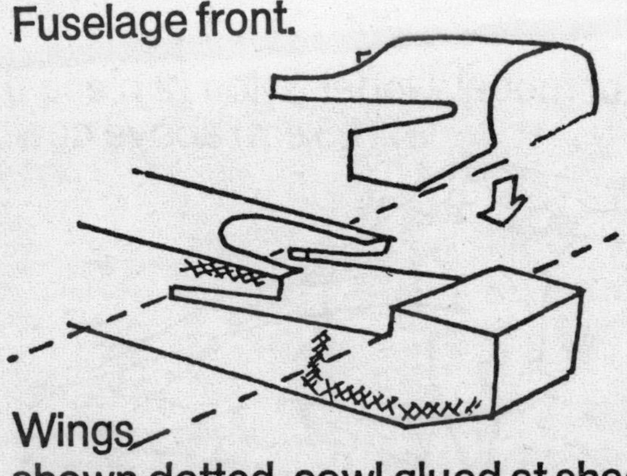

shown dotted, cowl glued at shaded area.

(6) The tailplane is fitted in the slots at the rear of the fuselage and the rudder, single thickness only, is glued in position with the shaded tab between the tailplane and the fuselage bottom.

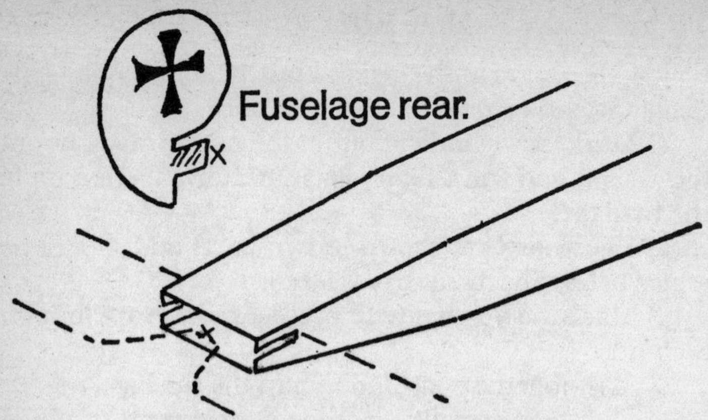

Tailplane shown dotted, rudder tab glued at point X.

(7) The undercarriage and pylon are made from $\frac{1}{16}$in (1.5mm) dowel and stiff bristle as shown in the diagram.

Front end of model. Upper pylon (2 pieces). ½″ (1.3 cm) above cowl.

Lower pylons (4 pieces). ½″ (1.3 cm) below fuselage. Undercarriage struts (2) ¾″ (1.9 cm).

(8) The rigging cotton can be made in two parts, starting from the front and rear of the undercarriage frame.

(9) The wheels are $\frac{11}{16}$in (17mm) diameter and cut from stiff card.

Propeller. Cut from card or balsa.

Engine cowl.

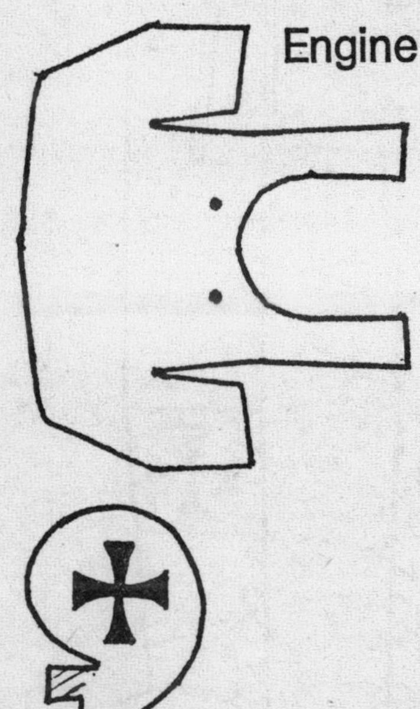

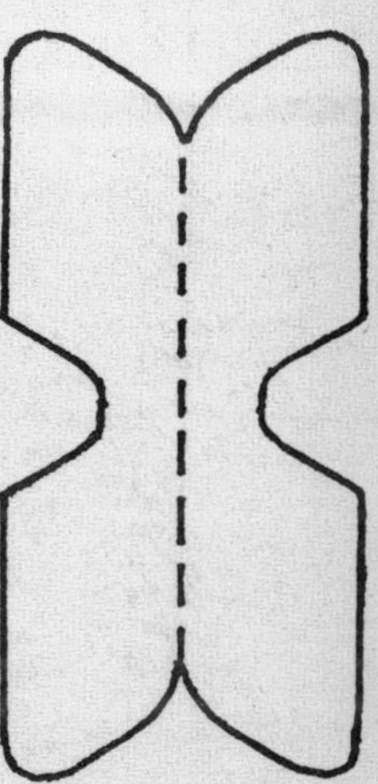

Rudder.
Cut from thicker card.

Tailplane.

Model Plans

Fuselage.
A
A
B
B
A
A
C
AAAA Lower pilot holes.
BB Undercarriage struts.
C Rear skid.

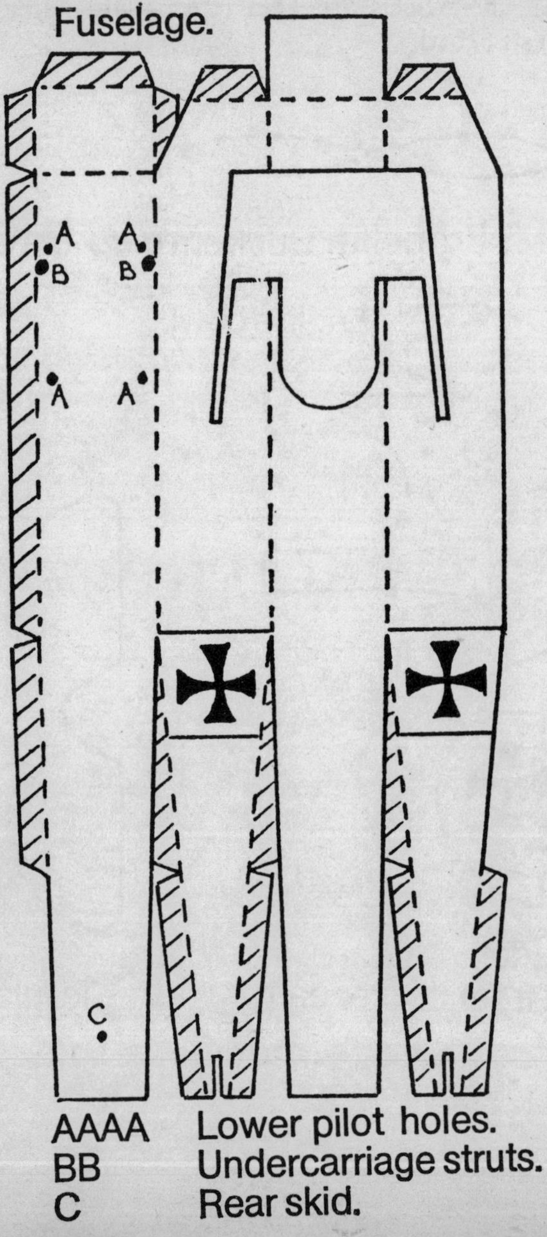

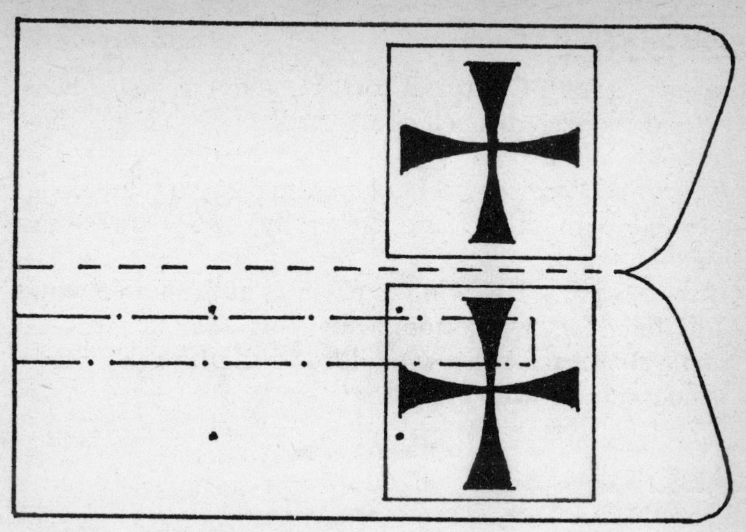

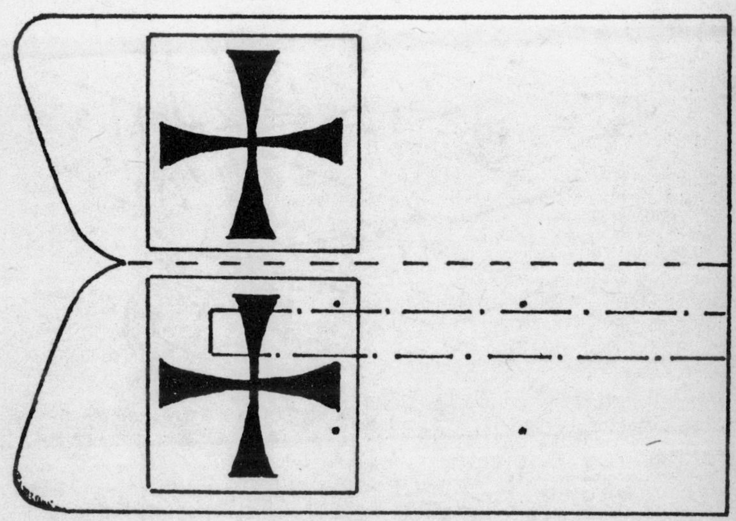

Wings. Join with card and one strip of balsa.

Fokker Dr I 'Triplane' — Germany 1918

Power 110hp Oberursel rotary engine driving a two-bladed wooden propeller about 8ft 6in (2.60m) diameter.

Fuselage Welded steel tube frame 19ft (5.8m) long covered with fabric and, generally, two Parabellum machine-guns.

Wings Span: Top wing 23ft 6in (7.0m); middle wing 20ft 6in (6.25m); bottom wing 18ft 10in (5.75m). A single strut each side gave added strength to the wings which were not wire braced.

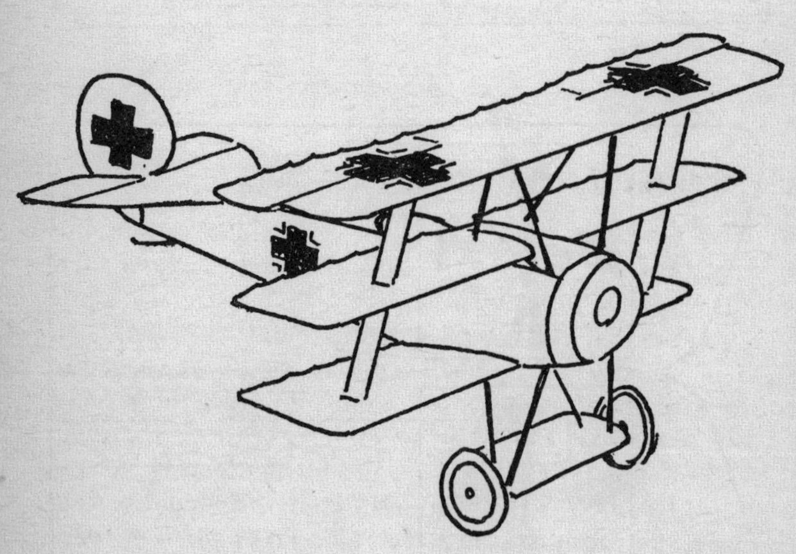

To Make the Fokker Dr I Triplane

Complete stages A and B. of the general instructions but first read the following details so that you understand the assembly procedure.

(1) Cut out and assemble fuselage in the normal way. The top section behind the cockpit should be curved to give the required 'rounded' shape. The section in front of the cockpit should be assembled without rounding and is the position for mounting the middle wing.

(2) To achieve the rounded shape of the engine cowl inserted a trimmed 'Smarties' tube lid or piece of balsa $\frac{13}{16}$in (21mm) diameter into the front of the fuselage during assembly.

(3) The fuselage top is glued in position after the wings have been attached and completes the circular shape of the engine cowl and front end of the body.

The engine fairing can now be glued in position.

(4) The undercarriage fairing should be glued with a $\frac{1}{16}$in (1.5mm) dowel or cocktail stick in position to serve as the axle. Gluing the rear edge only should give the right aerofoil section.

(5) Wheels. $\frac{5}{8}$in (16mm) diameter. Draw with a compass on stiff card and paint the tyres before fixing to the axle.

Follow Stage C and make up the three wings paying particular attention to the slots and holes for the struts. These are marked with shaded rectangles and black dots.

In the lower wing these are in the *top* surface only.
In the middle wing they are through *both* surfaces.
In the top wing they are only in the *lower* surface.

The dotted semi-circles in the middle wing can be removed.

Attach the middle wing first with the leading edge $\frac{3}{8}$in (10mm) from the front of the fuselage. Fix the lower wing in position, on the flat section of the body and leave both wings to dry making sure that they are square.

Cut out two pieces of $\frac{1}{16}$in × $\frac{3}{16}$in (5.0 × 1.5mm) balsa strip $1\frac{7}{8}$in (4.7mm) long and sand gently to remove corners. The ends should be cut slightly off square to give the forward rake to the wings.

When the two wings are dry the struts should be passed through the middle wing and glued in position in the lower and the middle wing.

The top wing is supported by the two main struts and four thinner ones in the centre. Ideal material for these four struts are the bristles of a stiff brush. Holes should be pierced in the fuselage and top of the middle wing with the compass in the positions shown on the plan. Glue the bristle struts into the fuselage, put a spot of glue into the two slots and the four holes in the upper wing and position the model into them. Support the whole assembly, being sure that it is in the correct position and leave to dry.

Mark and cut out the tailplane and rudder. The tailplane is folded to give a double thickness. The rudder is also folded and is glued together with the rear section of the fuselage sandwiched between the two sides.

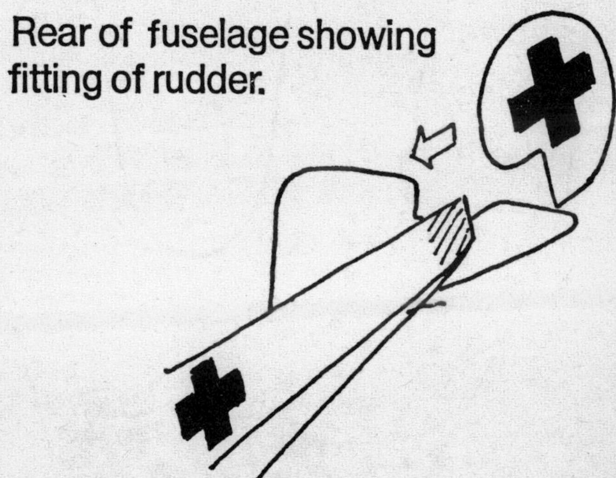

Various colour schemes were used on Dr I triplanes. The model looks very attractive in 'Red Baron' colours: bright red on all surfaces except the rudder which should be white and the underside of the plane which was pale blue. The markings are black crosses with a white border as shown on the plans.

Model Plans

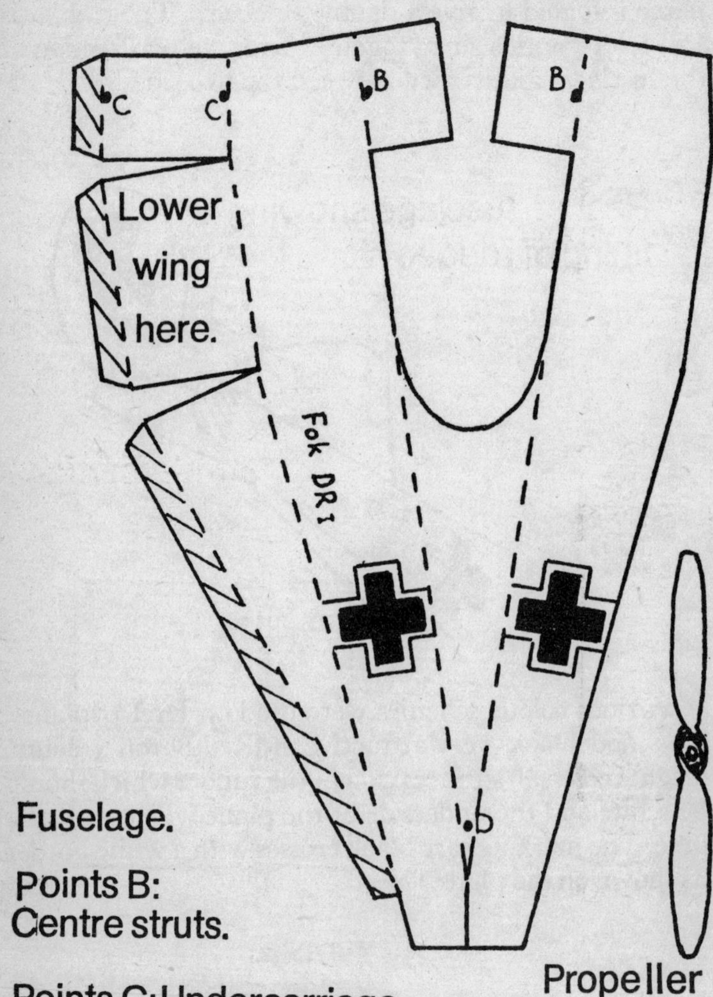

Points C: Undercarriage.
Front struts.

Point D: Skid.

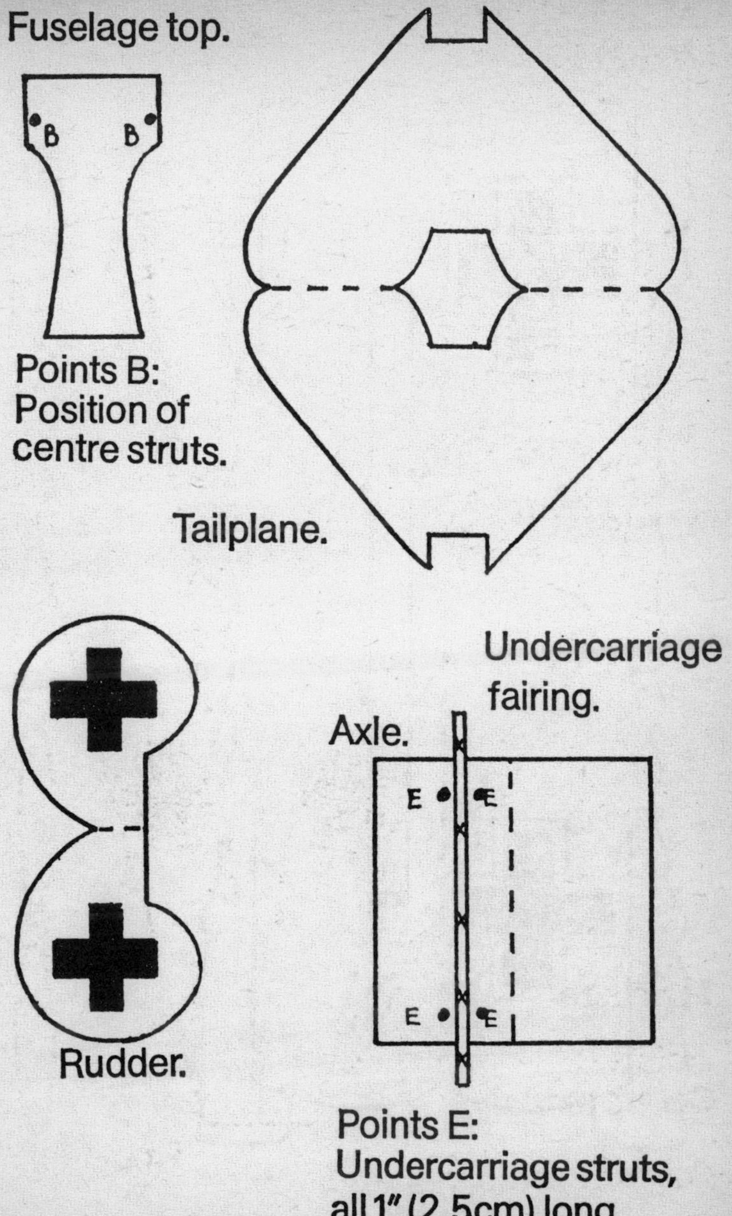

Points E:
Undercarriage struts,
all 1″ (2.5cm) long.

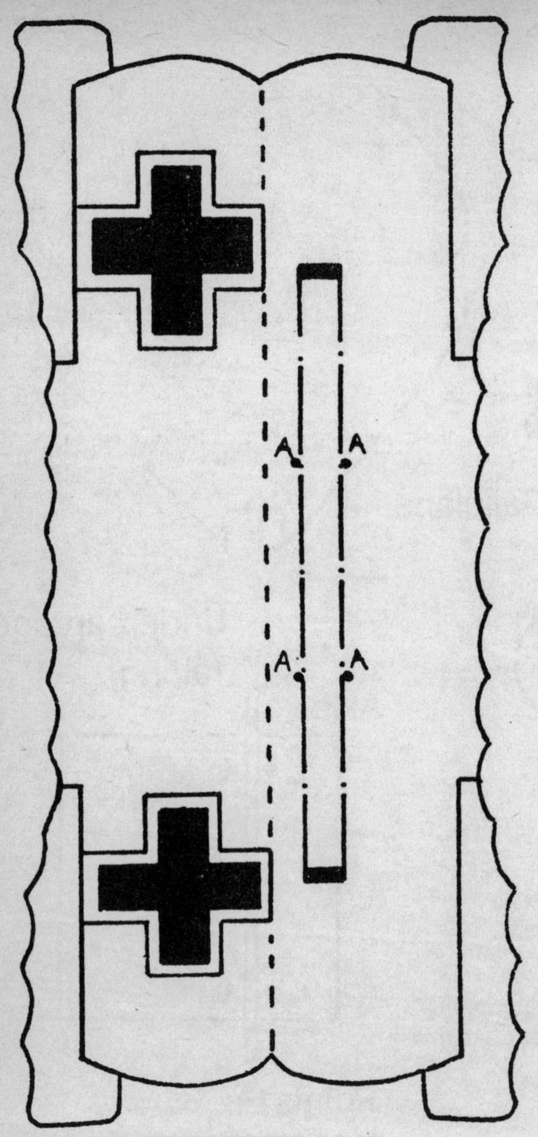

Top wing.
Points A: Position of centre struts.

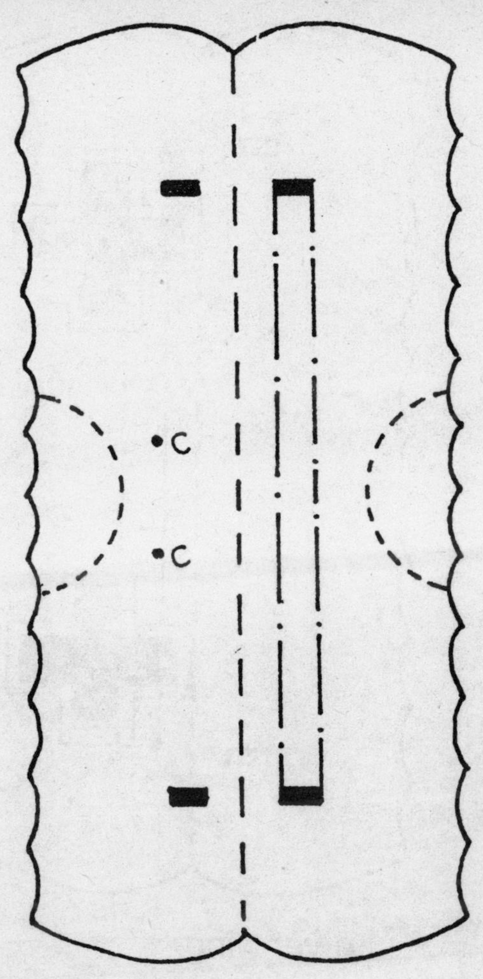

Middle wing.
Points C: centre struts.

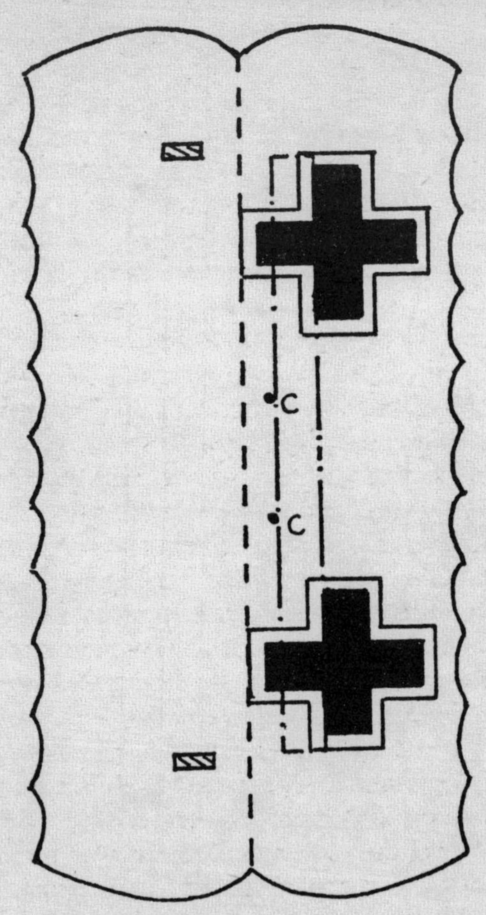

Lower wing.

Points C: undercarriage rear struts.

XX Sopwith

Sir Thomas Octave Murdoch Sopwith, the son of a wealthy engineer, was born in 1888 and educated in engineering. He was a very enthusiastic yachtsman but in 1910 became interested in the new sport of flying. He qualified as a pilot in November 1910, and within a few weeks had won the £4,000 prize for the longest flight by an Englishman to the Continent with a flight from England to Belgium, a distance of 169 miles (272km). In 1911 and 1912 he won several major races and established a flying school at Brooklands.

In 1912 he turned his attention to building aircraft of his own. The first two were modifications of existing machines but the third was a truly original design and was influenced by Sopwith's love of yachting. This machine was the first British hull-type flying boat and was later modified to become one of the first amphibious flying boats designed in Europe with the fitting of a retractable wheeled undercarriage.

Sopwith sold several machines to the Naval and Military wings of the R.F.C. and his planes continued to win important races flown by Harry Hawker. During the First World War the name Sopwith won lasting fame with many successful aircraft: the *Baby, Pup, Camel, Dolphin* and *Snipe*. This family of aircraft played a major role in Britain's war effort.

During the recession after the war Sopwith wound up his original company and formed Hawker Engineering Ltd. The new company maintained the Sopwith tradition and produced many excellent aircraft, the most famous was, perhaps the *Hurricane* of WW II.

In the years after the second war Sopwith's company became the giant of the British aircraft industry by buying up several other companies and Sir Thomas became the chairman of the Hawker Siddeley Group.

The Sopwith Pup

'*Pup*' was the unofficial name given to a single seat fighting scout built by the Sopwith Aviation Company during WW I. The name was used because the plane was very similar to the 2 seat '*1½ Struter*' but very much smaller. Though its engine was only 80hp its performance was remarkable and its handling qualities impeccable. A 100hp engine was fitted to some later models.

Pups went into service with the R.N.A.S. in the Autumn of 1916 and for a little more than a year proved that they were excellent fighting machines and were much in demand by pilots. The *Pup* was withdrawn from the Western Front by the end of 1917 but the model remained in production throughout 1918 and served mainly as a training machine.

In the Autumn of 1917 the Admiralty decided to equip all light cruisers and battle cruisers with a platform to allow aircraft to take off and land. The ships should carry fighting aeroplanes. *Pups* were built with sprung skids in place of wheels and arrester hooks to engage with cables across the deck to bring the plane to a rapid stop when landing.

Catapult tests were carried out for launching larger aircraft but these were abandoned, mainly because the *Pup* could operate from the small platforms without difficulty.

Sopwith 'Pup'. Fighting Scout Britain 1916–1918

Power 80hp or 100hp rotary air-cooled engine driving a wooden two-bladed propeller 8ft 6in (2.60m) diameter.

Fuselage Wire braced ash and spruce box girder 19ft 4in (5.9m) long. The top was covered in plywood, the front and engine were covered in aluminium and the rest in fabric.

Wings Span: 26ft 6in (7.9m) Brazed steel tube and wooden frame covered in fabric. The wings were wire-braced and connected by struts.

Most *Pups* had a single Vickers gun mounted centrally on the fuselage immediately ahead of the cockpit.

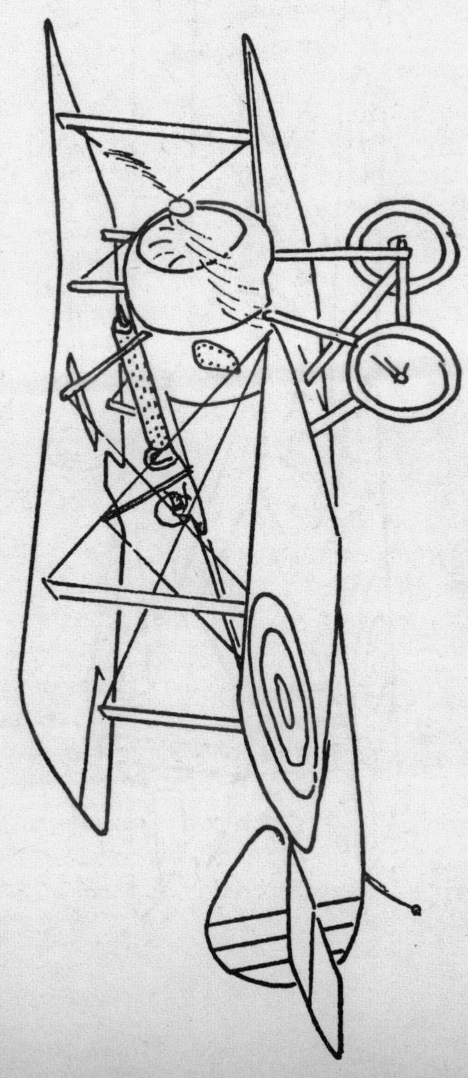

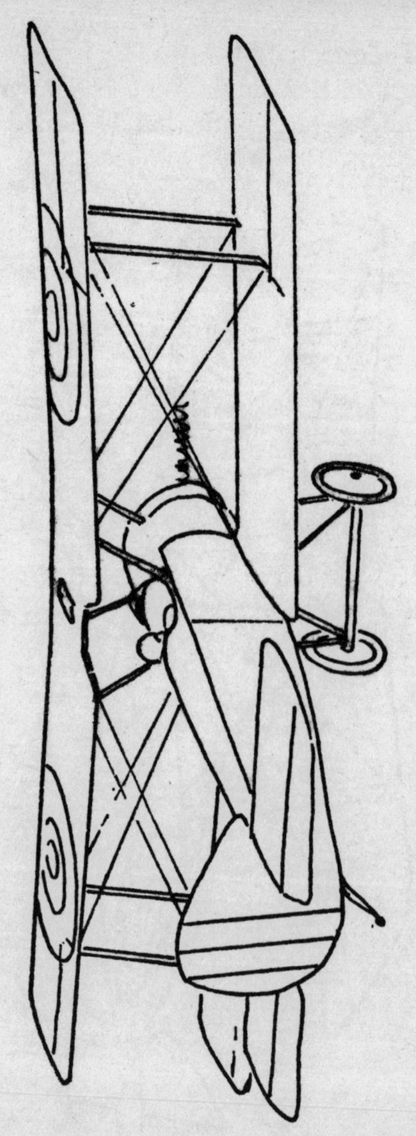

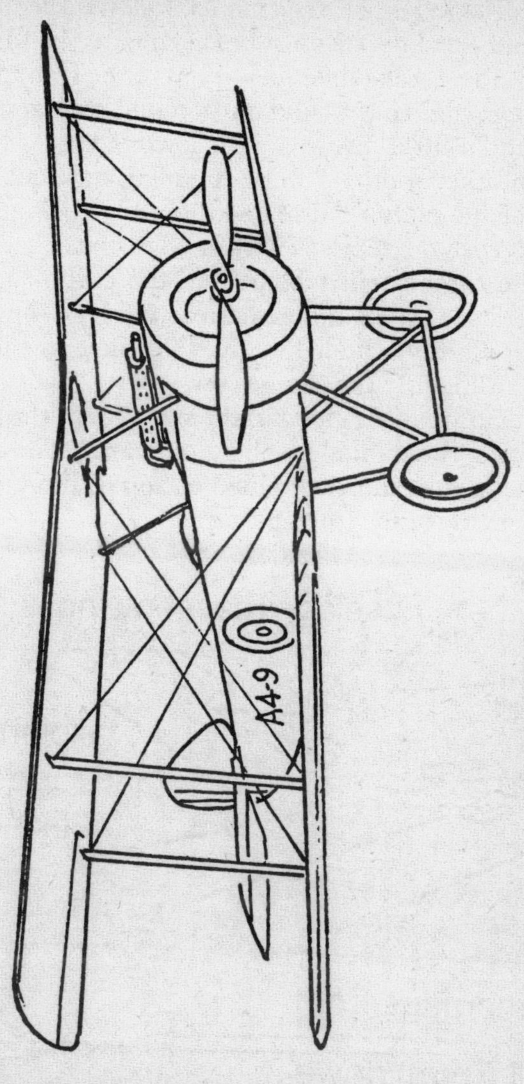
A4-9

To Make the Sopwith Pup

(1) Construction of this model follows the normal pattern but special care must be taken with the fuselage. Note that the scoring lines do not run to the front edge of the fuselage and that a solid cutting line runs across the bottom and a little way along the lower edges of it. This is to allow the front end to be rounded, not square like the rest of the body. You may cut out the cockpit opening if you wish but leave the heavy edge line.

(2) The three small tabs behind the cockpit are not scored and are glued under the rear fuselage top which should be slightly rounded to give the whole top a gentle curve blending into the engine cowling.

(3) The tailplane is glued to the two tabs at the rear of the fuselage, these should be bent outwards. The rudder should be folded and then glued on top of the tailplane and either side of the fuselage.

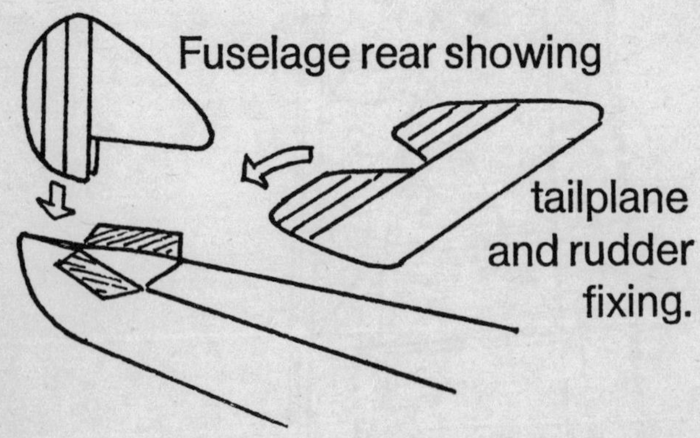

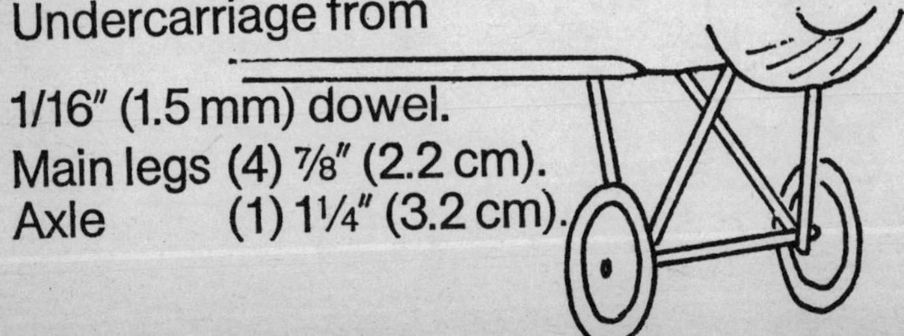

(4) The lower main wings are cut out in one piece and assembled with two balsa strips; remember to cut out the strut slots. The completed wing is then glued in position. The top wing is made with two balsa strips, the wider one having a piece removed to allow the hole to be cut in the wing to give the pilot a view above him. The upper wing is supported by four main struts $1\frac{1}{4}$in (3.2cm) long cut from $\frac{1}{4}$in × $\frac{1}{16}$in (6.0 × 1.5mm) balsa lightly sanded to remove the corners. The ends should be cut at an angle to allow the top wing to be placed forward of the lower one. The centre section is supported by four thin struts glued in position.

(5) The undercarriage is made from $\frac{1}{16}$in (1.5mm) dowel as shown in the diagram, the wheels, cut from thicker card, are $\frac{9}{16}$in (1.1cm) diameter.

(6) Finish the front of the fuselage with a piece of soft balsa cut to fit inside the rounded nose and sanded to the shape of the cowl.

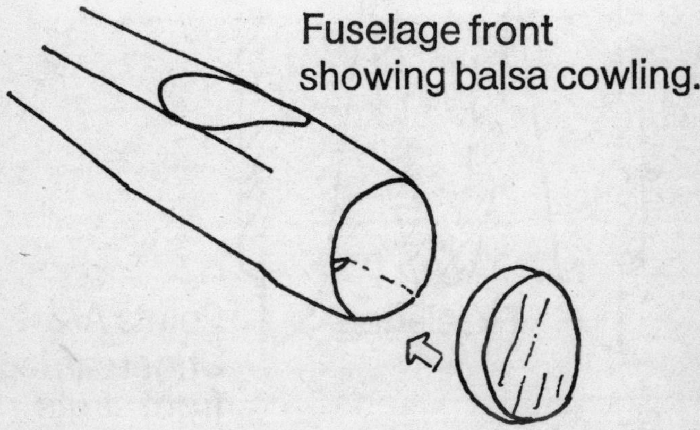

(7) The gun, propeller and bracing wires can now be fitted.

(8) Paint the sides and bottom surfaces beige and the upper surfaces dark brown. The engine cowl should be aluminium and the rudder and elevator red, white and blue stripes.

Model Plans

A
A
Fuselage.
Points AA:
Undercarriage
front struts.
B
W
R
Rudder.
B – Blue
W – White
R – Red

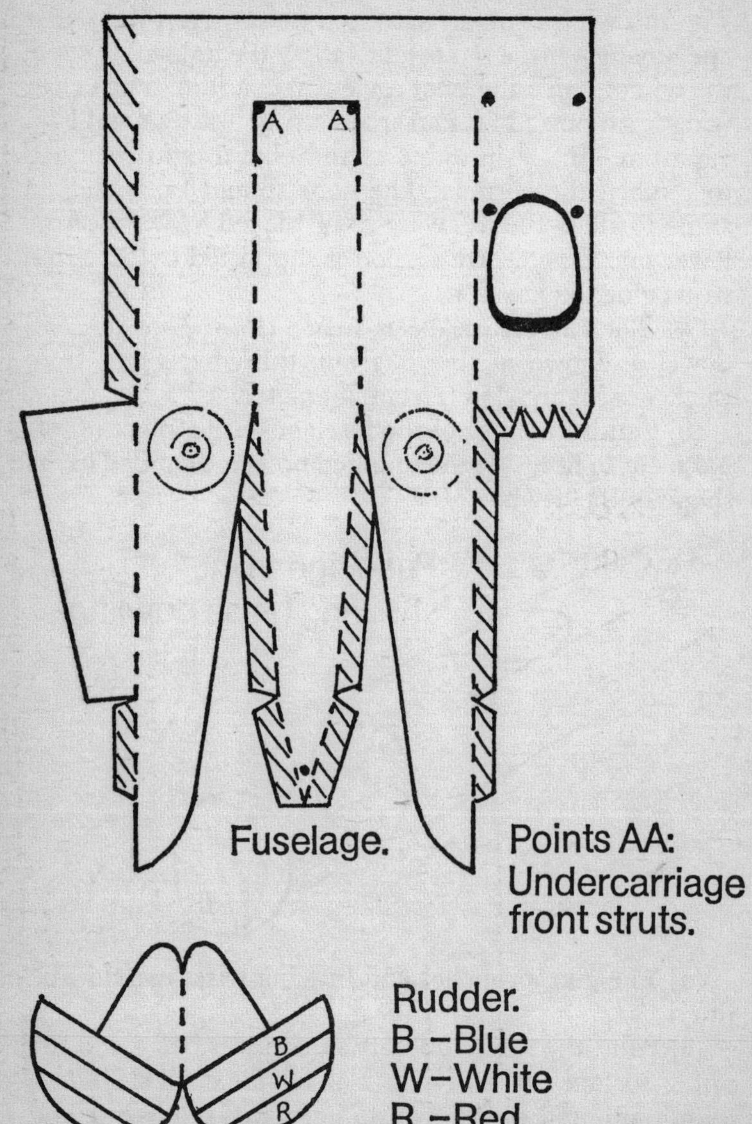

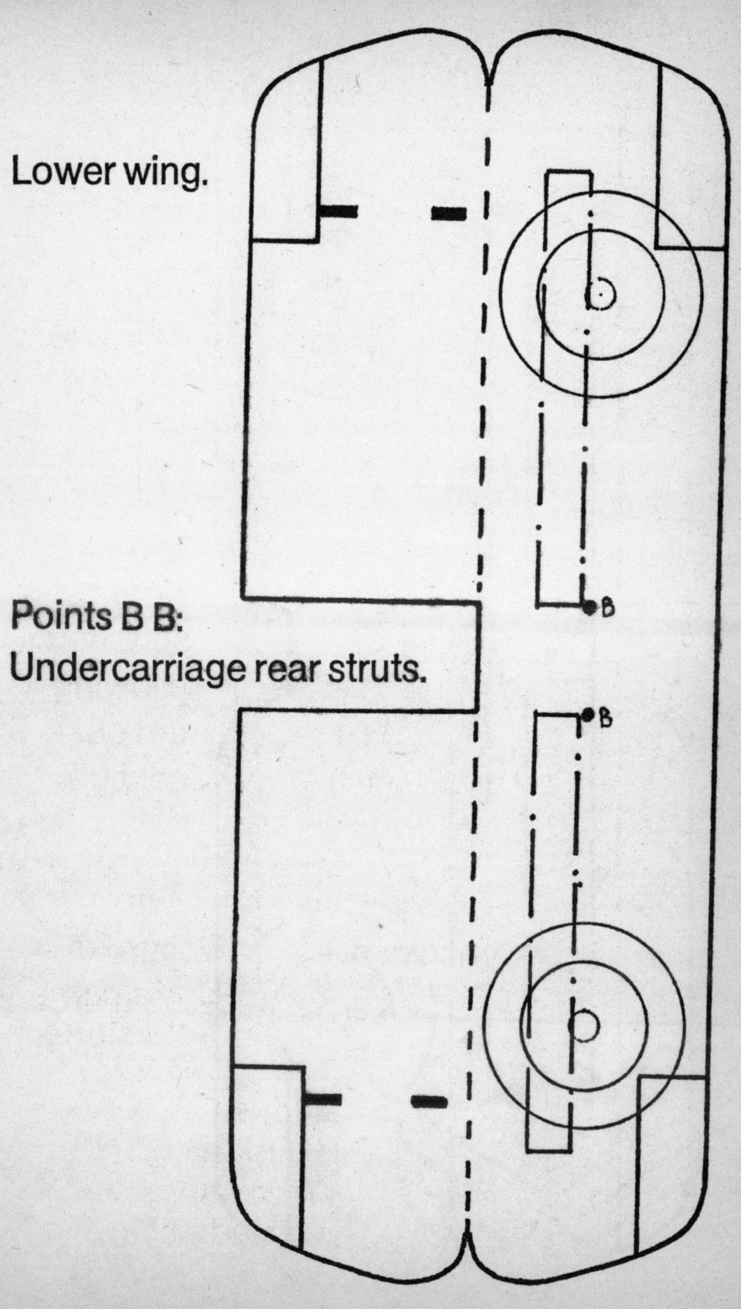
Lower wing.
B
B
Points B B:
Undercarriage rear struts.

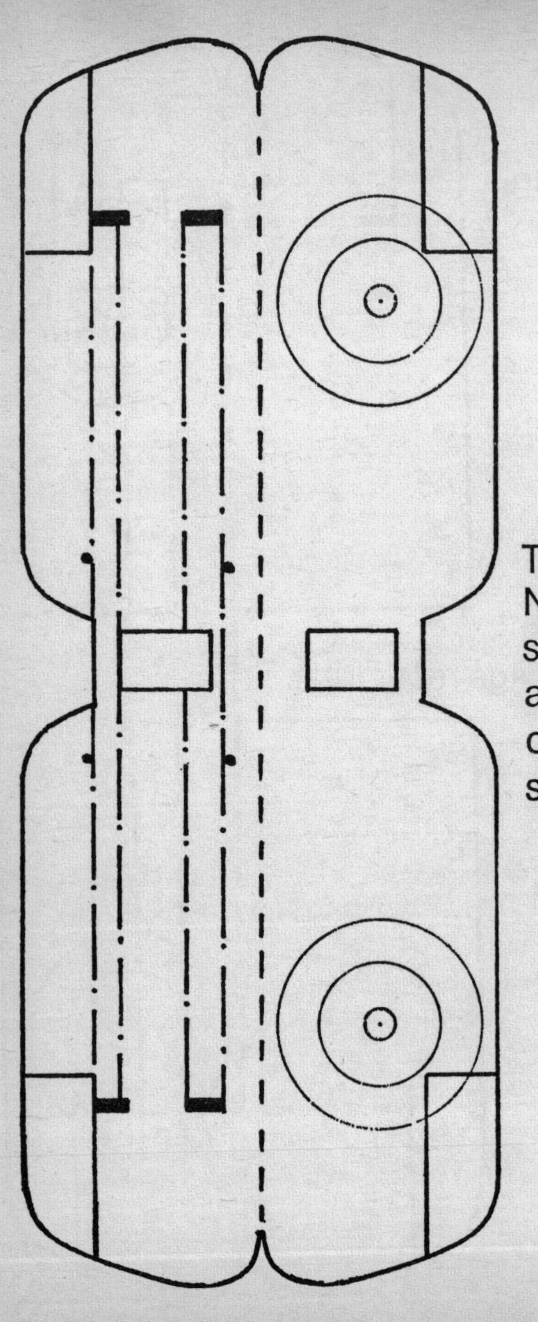

Top wing. Note balsa stiffeners· allowing cut out section.

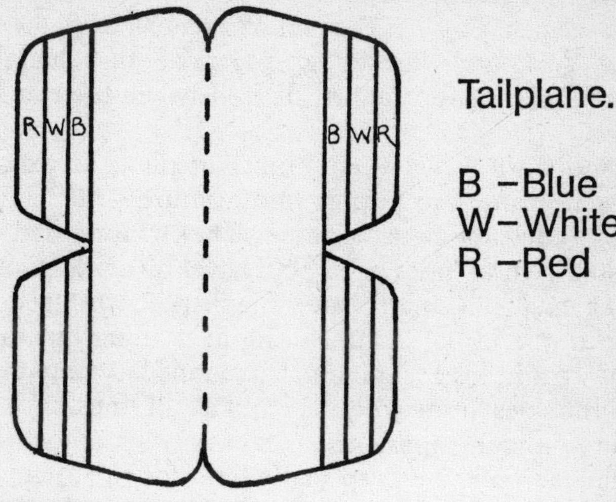

Tailplane.

B –Blue
W–White
R –Red

Propeller.

Cut from stiff card or balsa.

Spirit of St. Louis

At the age of 25 Charles Lindbergh won his place among the great pioneer pilots. On the 21st May, 1927, he landed in Paris at the end of a 33½ hour flight from New York and won a $25,000 prize that had been offered in 1920 for the first flight between the two great cities.

Lindbergh was a very competent pilot, an excellent navigator and had a spirit of adventure – all the qualities needed for his epic flight. The Atlantic had been crossed several times before but never by a solo pilot and never in such a small plane. Lindbergh was faced with loneliness and boredom, staring at nothing but the instruments in his cockpit and surrounded by only the sea and the skies for nearly a day and a half must have been a very difficult experience.

The aeroplane was specially built for the attempt by the Ryan Airlines Company, officially designated Ryan NYP (New York–Paris) and christened *Spirit of St. Louis*. It was almost a flying fuel tank with an engine and a cockpit – the body and wings held 450 gallons (1,705 litres) of fuel and the only forward view that the pilot had was through a periscope. The plane first flew on the 27th April, 1927, and was then prepared for the Atlantic attempt.

With the tanks filled with fuel the aircraft was so heavy that it was not certain that it would even leave the ground but it did struggle into the air and started on its epic flight.

Charles Lindbergh returned to the United States with the *Spirit of St. Louis* and toured the country in an attempt to create public interest in civil airline development. In 1929 Lindbergh married and in the following years the couple flew on several airline surveys for Pan

American, covering the North and South Atlantic and the North Pacific routes.

Ryan NYP. Spirit of St. Louis U.S.A. 1927

Power One 237hp Wright J-5C Whirlwind 9-cylinder radial engine driving a two-bladed metal propeller.
Fuselage Length 27ft 8in (8.43m).
Wings Span 46ft (14.0m).

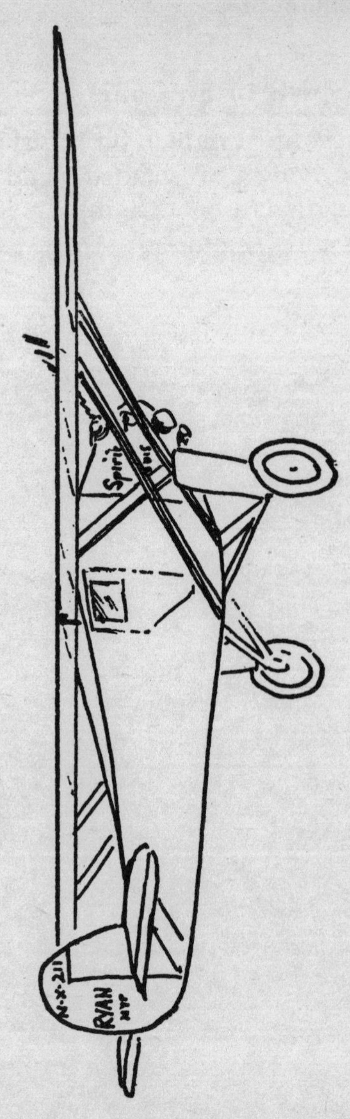
Spirit
N-X-211
RYAN

To Make the Ryan NYP*

This is probably the easiest model in the book as it is quite big and has no difficult curves.

(1) Start by marking, scoring and cutting out the fuselage. This comes in two parts, the smaller one being the top.

(2) Be sure to cut out the slots under the rudder for the tailplane and the four strut positions.

(3) When assembling the fuselage start with the underside. When this is dry, glue the two sides of the rudder together and then glue all the tabs for the top and fix it in position. The four tabs in the nose should be doubled back and glued into the front of the body.

(4) Only one wing is shown. Cut out a pair marking one opposite to the other. Assemble the two halves with a piece of card glued over the joint and the balsa strip in position. When dry the complete wing can be glued in place.

(5) The wing struts are cut from $\frac{1}{16}$in × $\frac{3}{16}$in (1.5 × 4.5mm) balsa 3in (7.6cm) long and sanded lightly to remove the corners. Put a little glue on each end of the strut, push into the fuselage hole and then slide into position in the slot in the wing.

(6) Cut out the undercarriage and double over the two Vee sections to strengthen the legs, the triangular sections should have been removed from the other half.

(7) The centre section is then glued under the fuselage with the folded part forward and underneath the front wing strut.

(8) Another piece of $\frac{1}{16}$in × $\frac{3}{16}$in (1.5 × 4.5mm) balsa 1$\frac{1}{16}$in (2.7cm) long is then glued between the top of the fuselage and the front strut on each side.

(9) From below the joint on the strut, a piece of balsa, again with the edges rounded, $\frac{1}{8}$in × $\frac{3}{8}$in (3.0 × 10.0mm) and $\frac{3}{4}$in (1.9cm) long is glued between the

strut and the undercarriage leg leaving the end of the leg turned down to take the wheel. The wheels $\frac{3}{4}$in (1.9cm) diameter should be made from thick card and glued in position.

(10) The tailplane should be prepared and glued into position.

(11) To finish the front of the aeroplane use a piece of soft balsa carved to fit into the rounded nose and cut to the shape of the spinner.

(12) Nine small pieces of balsa should then be glued around the front of the fuselage to represent the cylinders of the radial engine and the two propeller blades fitted, unless you wish to display the model in the air.

(13) Paint the model silver blue with the engine cowl aluminium.

Front of model

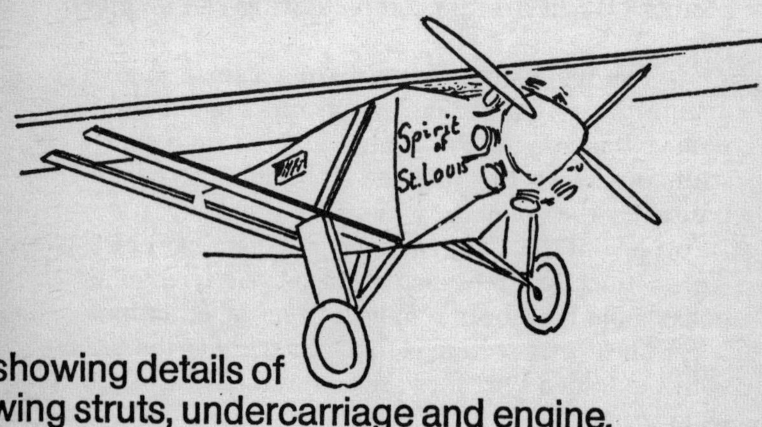

showing details of
wing struts, undercarriage and engine.

Propeller blade. Make two from thick card or balsa and glue into spinner.

Spirit of St. Louis
Spirit of St. Louis
RYAN N.Y.P.
N-X-211
RYAN N.Y.P.
N-X-211

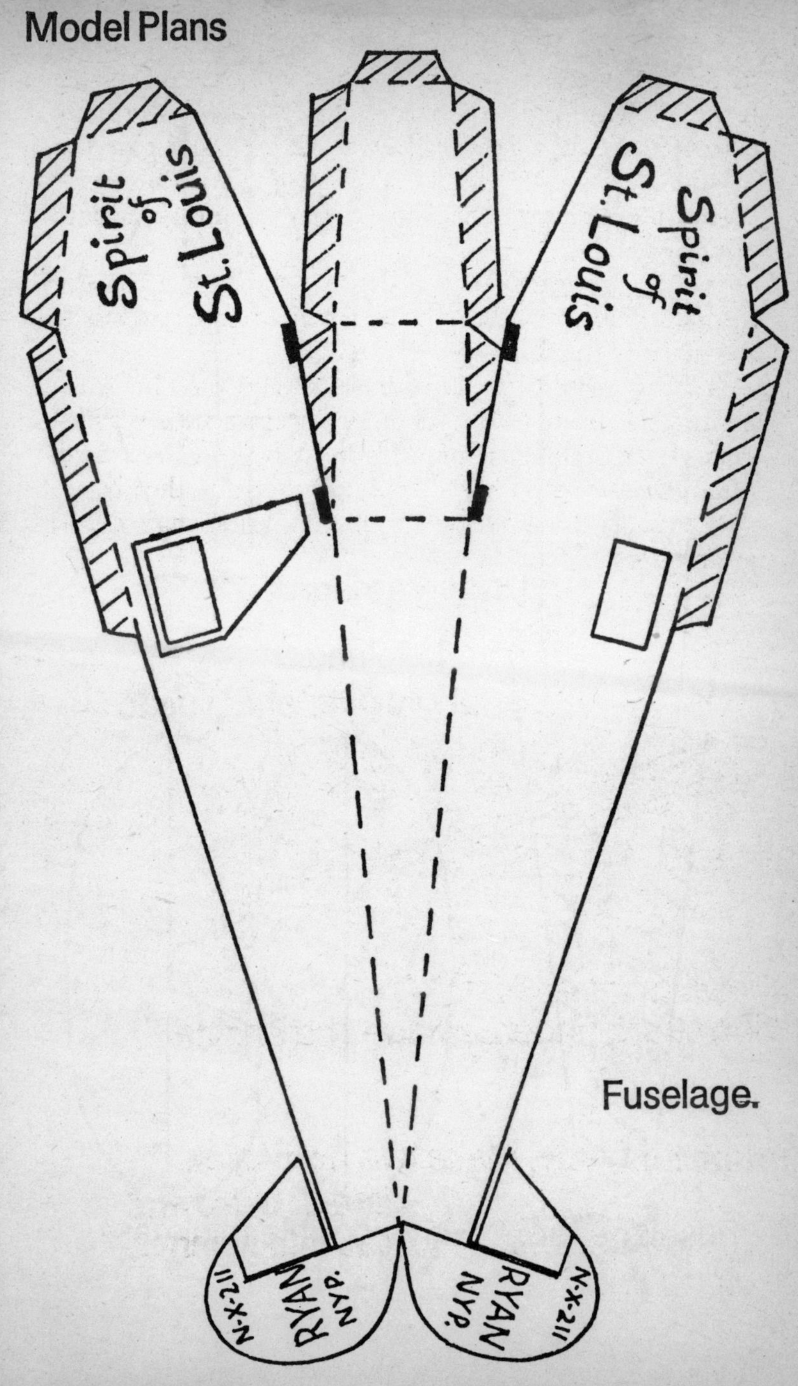

Fuselage.

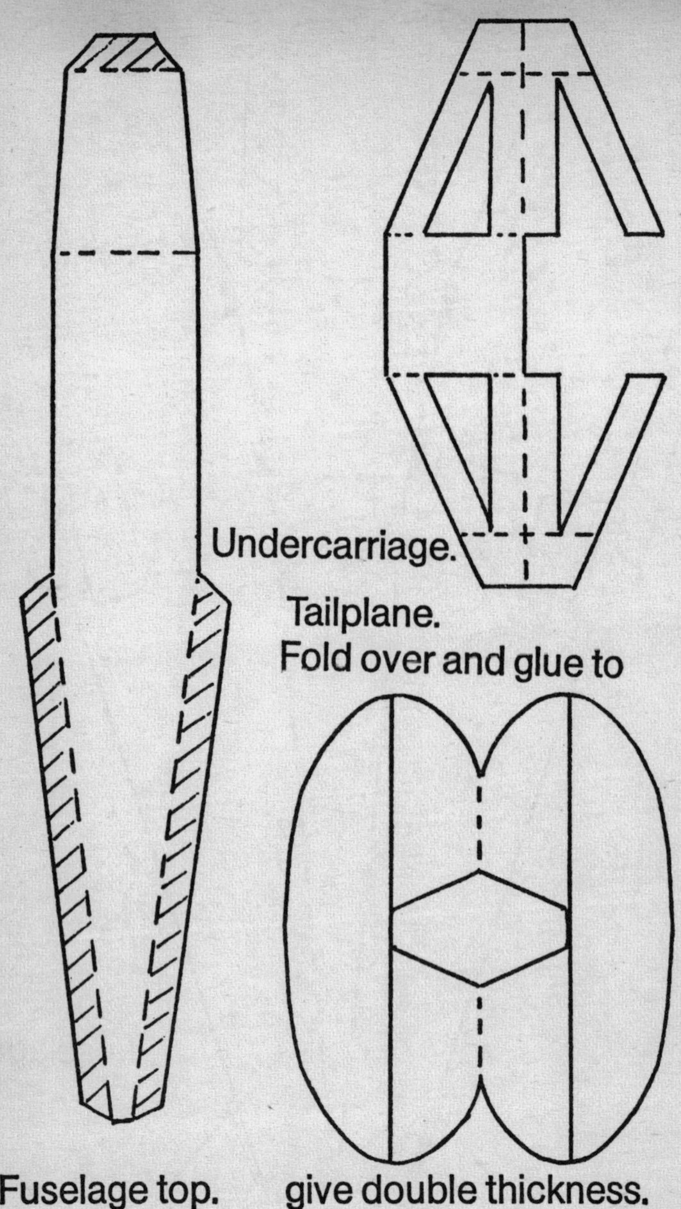
Undercarriage.
Tailplane.
Fold over and glue to
Fuselage top.
give double thickness.

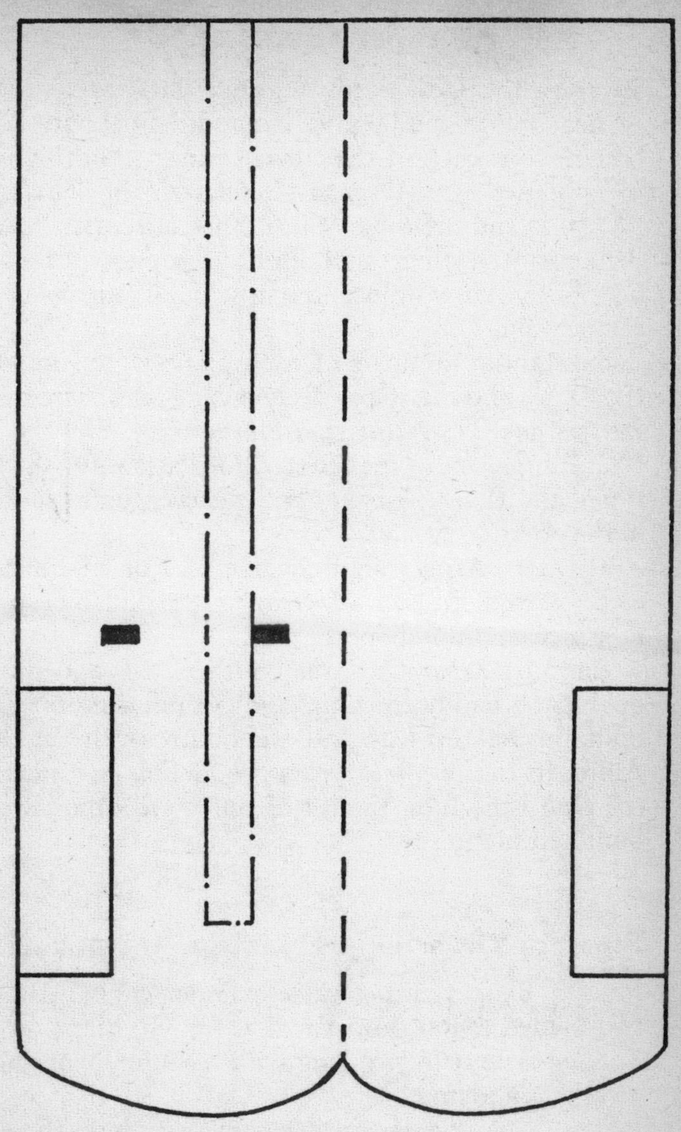

Wing.
Cut out two and join together with card and balsa strip.

Piper Grasshopper

In 1941 the U.S. Army selected three types of light planes for trials in observation and liaison duties. They bought four each of the current commercial high-wing monoplanes, the *Aeronca 'Defender'*, the *Taylorcraft Model D* and the *Piper 'Cub'*. These aircraft effectively demonstrated their usefulness in support of ground actions by Army units and as a very fast means of communication.

Substantial numbers of each plane were supplied to the Army and many privately owned ones were drafted into service. The Army gave all the aeroplanes the name *Grasshopper* and type letter *L* for liaison. Of the three types, the *Piper Grasshopper* was eventually produced in the greatest numbers.

To meet Army requirements, various modifications were carried out and the *Grasshoppers* gave very valuable service throughout the war.

The first *Piper Cub* was built in 1938 and by 1941 over 5,500 had been completed, a similar number were built during the war and went into service with the Allies. In the post-war years production continued and the *Cub* is high on the list of the world's most widely-built aeroplanes.

Piper L4 'Grasshopper' Liaison. U.S.A. 1941

Power 65hp Continental 4-cylinder engine driving a two-bladed metal propeller 6.7ft (2.0m) diameter.
Fuselage 22ft (6.7m) long with seats for pilot and observer in tandem.
Wings Span: 35ft 3in (10.75m) mounted above the cockpit, the centre section is glazed to give the pilot and observer more visibility.

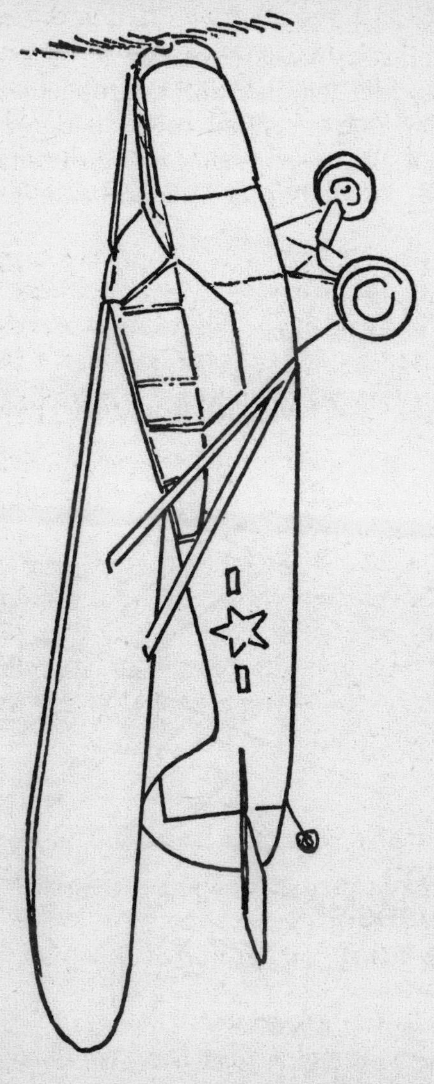

To Make the Piper Grasshopper

Providing you take care marking out this model it is not very difficult to assemble.

(1) The fuselage is made in one piece. Glue the two halves of the rudder together and the fuselage top first. When this is dry glue the engine cowl top and then bend the fuselage bottom to shape and glue in position. The end of this piece should be glued under the top section.

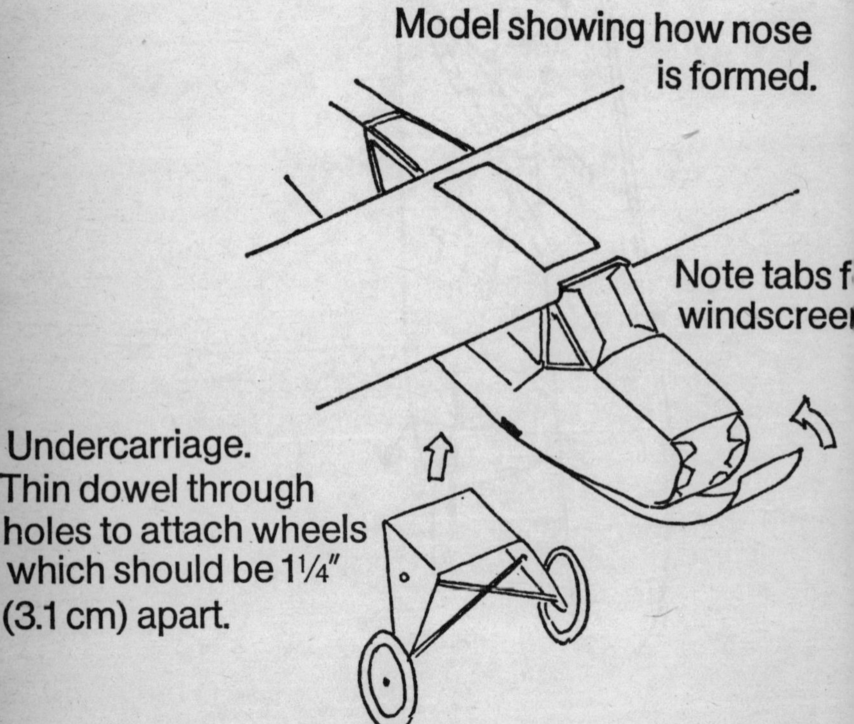

(2) The windscreen should be glued to the side tabs and behind the engine cowling.

(3) Only one half of the wing is shown, cut out two and stick together with a piece of card over the joint (on the inside of the wing) and one piece of balsa strip. Glue the wing to the tabs above the cockpit.

(4) The struts are made from $\frac{3}{16}$in × $\frac{1}{16}$in (1.5 × 4.5mm) balsa lightly sanded to remove the edges, $2\frac{3}{8}$in (6.0cm) long. Taper one side of each piece at the fuselage end and glue into place to form a vee.

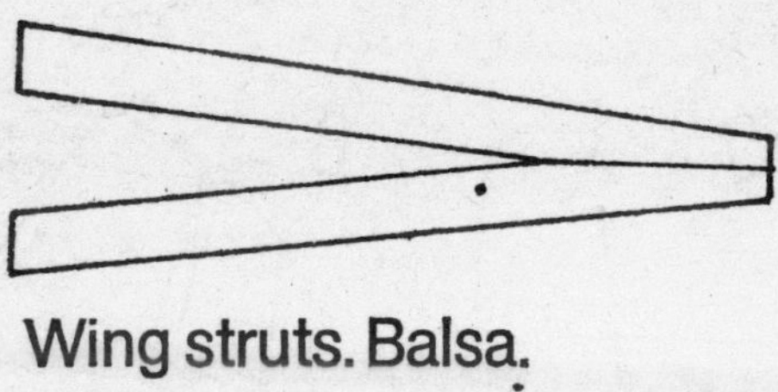

Wing struts. Balsa.

(5) The undercarriage is cut out and formed to shape and glued in position with the folded edge forward.

(6) The wheels $\frac{3}{8}$in (9mm) diameter should be out from thicker card and glued in position.

(7) Fit the tailplane into place and glue up the cut in the rudder. (8) Fit the propeller if you wish and then paint the model, pale blue underneath and light brown/green above.

Propeller.
Cut from stiff card or balsa.

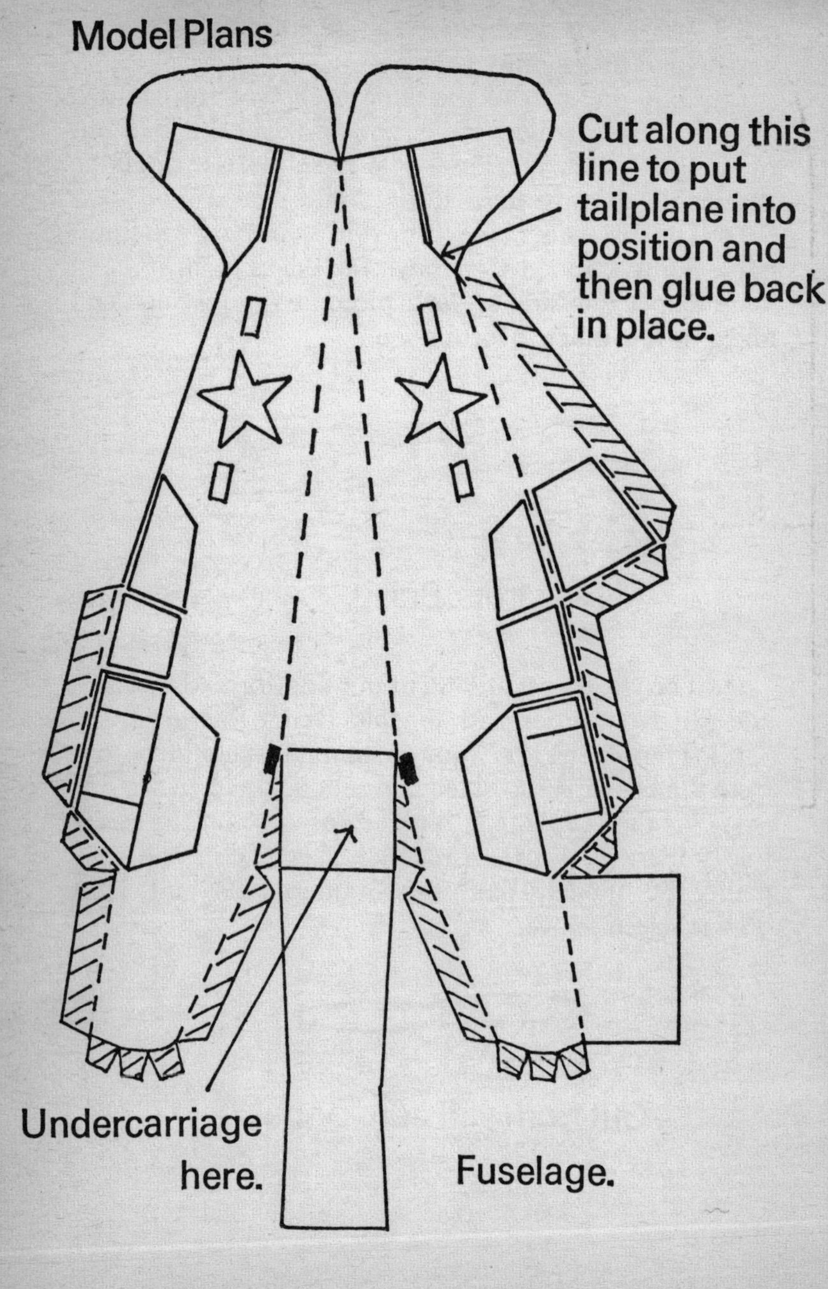
Model Plans
Cut along this line to put tailplane into position and then glue back in place.
Undercarriage here.
Fuselage.

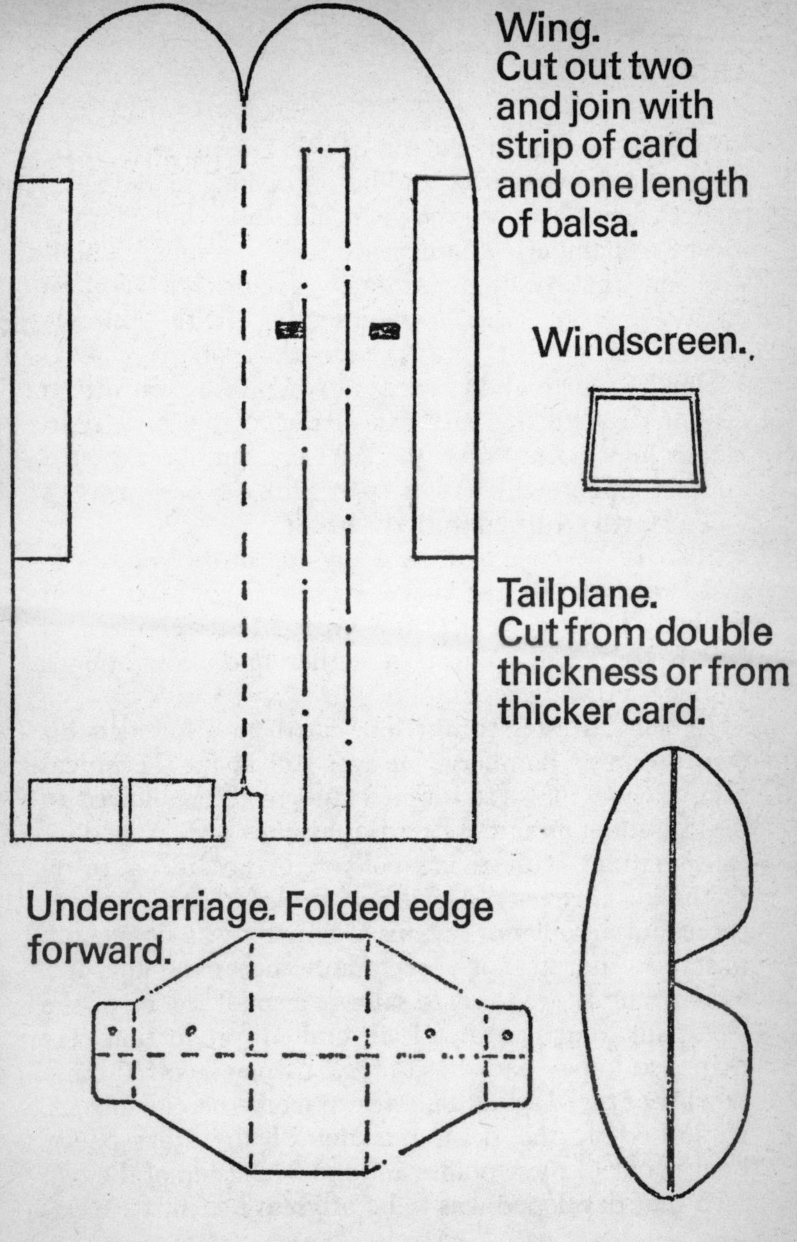
Wing.
Cut out two and join with strip of card and one length of balsa.
Windscreen.
Tailplane.
Cut from double thickness or from thicker card.
Undercarriage. Folded edge forward.

Willy Messerschmitt, the son of a Frankfurt wine merchant, was born in 1898 and began making model aeroplanes when he was eleven years old. In 1910 the family moved to Bamberg, 30 miles north of Nuremberg and it was here that Willy got to know Freidrich Harth, an Architect who was experimenting with full-size gliders.

Harth's fourth glider was built when Willy was fifteen years old. With the outbreak of the First World War, Harth joined the army and Messerschmitt completed another glider which was successfully flown in 1915 when Harth returned from the Front.

In 1917 Willy joined the army and at the end of the war became a student at the Technical High School in Munich. During the next few years Messerschmitt and Harth continued to work together and their designs gained a growing reputation.

In 1923 Messerschmitt left Harth and founded his own group at Bamberg. He was still at the Technical High School and was the first student to be allowed to build a glider as a major part of his thesis. He passed his examinations with flying colours to become a fully-qualified engineer. Messerschmitt produced several successful aeroplanes but his Company was financially unstable and in 1931 eventually became bankrupt. Messerschmitt was able to salvage a small section of the Company and continued in limited production. He managed to pay back most of the money he owed quite quickly as his *M23* light plane was a commercial success. Rudolf Hess, the deputy leader of the Nazi party, bought one of these planes and the friendship of the two men that developed was to be of great benefit to Messerschmitt when the Nazi party came to power in 1933 and his Company took over a new factory.

The benefit was short-lived as Messerschmitt's long standing enemy, Erhard Milch, was appointed Secretary of State for Air and orders for new aircraft were given to the rival Heinkel Company. Messerschmitt carried on, however, and tried to sell his planes abroad. At this time the first all-metal aircraft was built by the Company, this was the *Bf108* which gained many international records.

In 1935 Messerschmitt's most famous plane, the *Bf109* was first flown and it was this model which was to become one of the Luftwaffe's greatest fighter planes of World War II. Modifications and developments were made throughout the war and the type *109E* was built in the greatest numbers and gained a very good reputation in the hands of the German Fighter Pilots.

Messerschmitt 109E **Germany WW II**

Power Mercedes-Benz inverted Vee DB601A engine giving 985hp driving a three-bladed propeller. 9ft 3in (2.9m) diameter.

Fuselage 28ft 2in (8.58m) long with single seat cockpit.

Wings Span 32ft 4in (9.85m) with either four MG 17 machine-guns or, in later models, two MG FF cannon mounted in the leading edge.

Until May 1940 the Messerschmitt gave the Luftwaffe supremacy in the skies of Europe but over Dunkirk they met their match, the Spitfire.

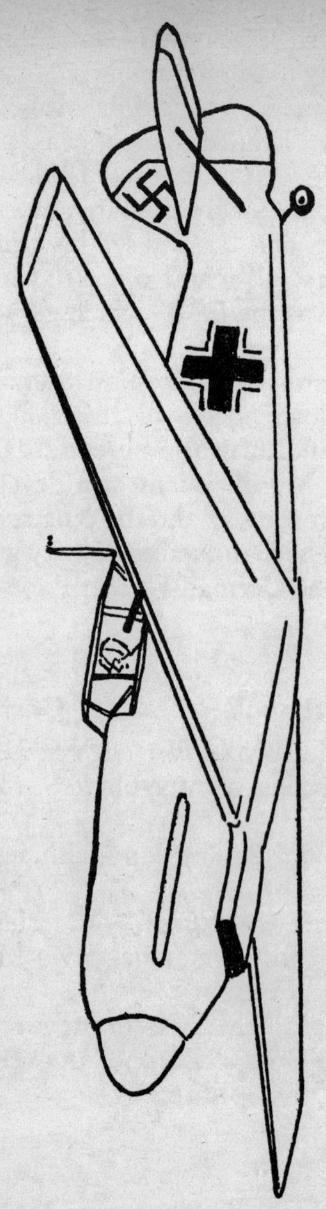

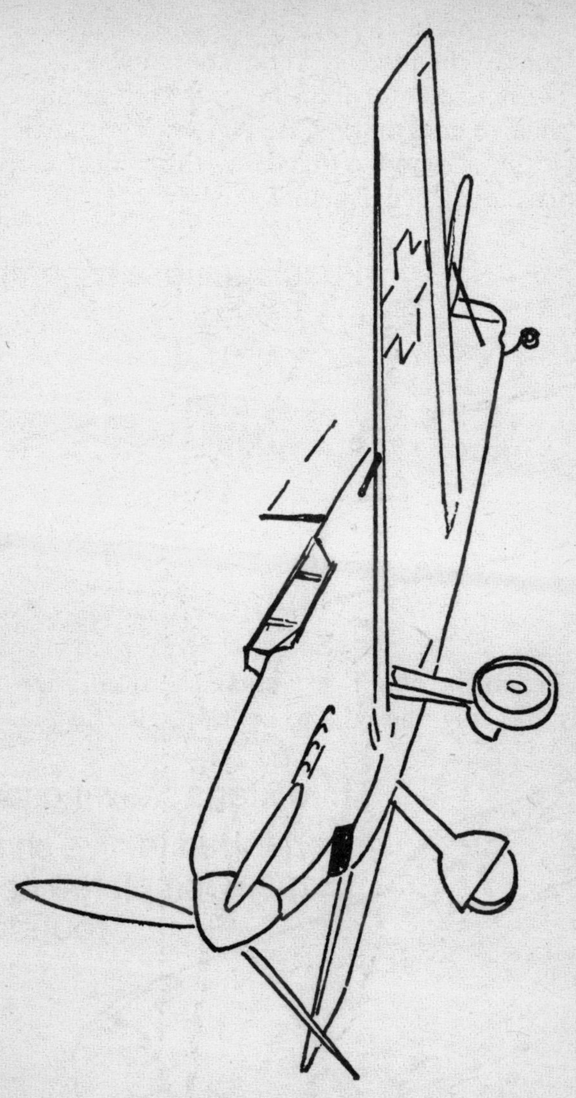

To Make the Messerschmitt Bf 109E

Assembly of this model is quite straightforward.

(1) Cut out the fuselage in the normal way.

(2) Do not score or fold line A B and be sure to cut along the five lines marked A. The fuselage, particularly at the front, is round so to achieve the correct shape roll the card round a pencil before gluing.

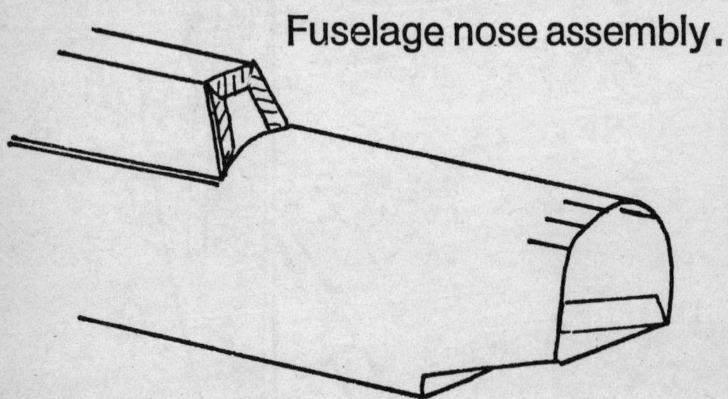

Fuselage nose assembly.

(3) When the glue is dry curve the front edge downwards allowing the cuts to overlap, glue in place and

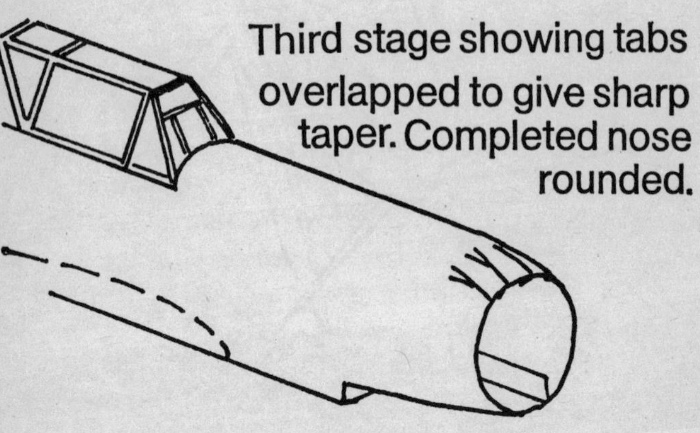

Third stage showing tabs overlapped to give sharp taper. Completed nose rounded.

cover the outside with glue to fill in the bumps and give a smooth rounded shape.

(4) Before gluing the two halves of the rudder together cut out the tailplane from thicker card or a double thickness of the normal card. Fixing the tailplane and rudder into the fuselage must be completed in one operation.

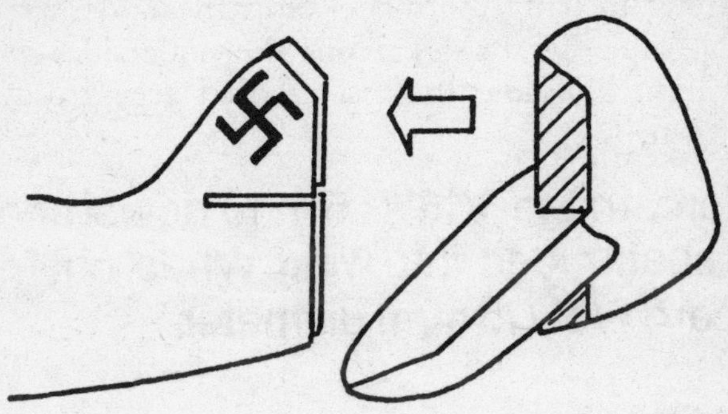

Tailplane and rudder glued between the two sides of the fuselage.

(5) The rudder, folded, glued and with the tailplane slot cut out, should be glued to the tailplane and then both fixed into the rear of the fuselage between the two halves of the rudder which should have been glued. The whole assembly should then be checked for accuracy and left to dry.

(6) Only one half of the wing is shown, cut out two, remembering to mark one opposite to the other. The balsa strip should be fixed only in the position shown. When both halves of the wing are assembled they are fixed to the fuselage with the trailing edge at the point C. The flat section under the fuselage in front of the wings is the air intake.

(7) To finish the model fit the cockpit front, glued to the tabs and fitted behind the curved engine cowling.

(8) Round the front end of the fuselage and cut the spinner from soft balsa, glue into place and fit the propeller blades.

(9) Cut out and assemble the undercarriage and fix in position.

In flight, the undercarriage would be retracted so if you intend to hang the model omit the undercarriage and the propeller blades. Paint the undersides of the model light blue and the rest mottled grey-green and dark green.

Undercarriage. 1/16″ (1.5 mm) dowel and card spats glued into wing. Wheel cut from stiff card 5/8″ (15 mm) diameter.

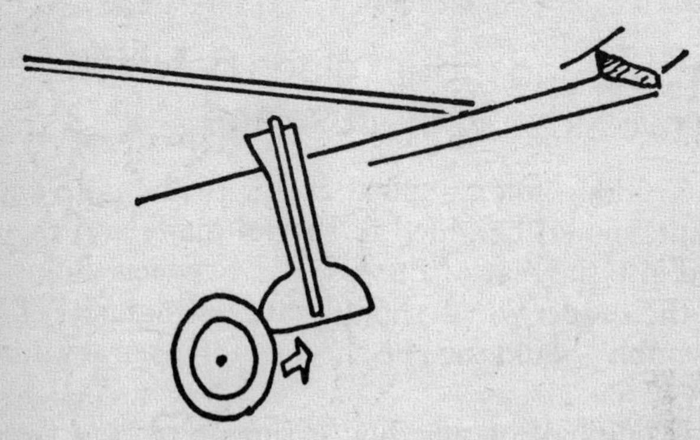

Model Plans

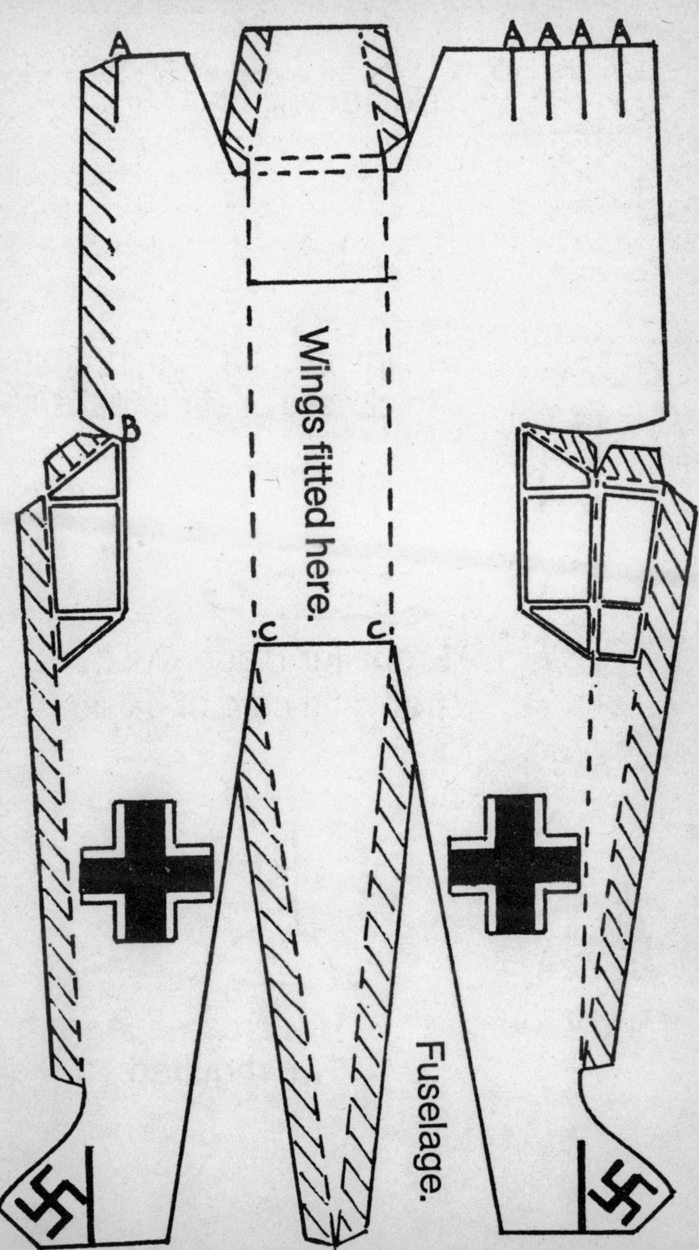

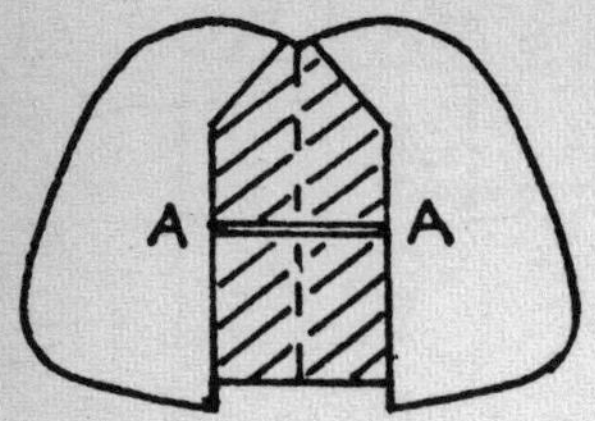

Rudder. Fold over to cut slot for tailplane (AA).

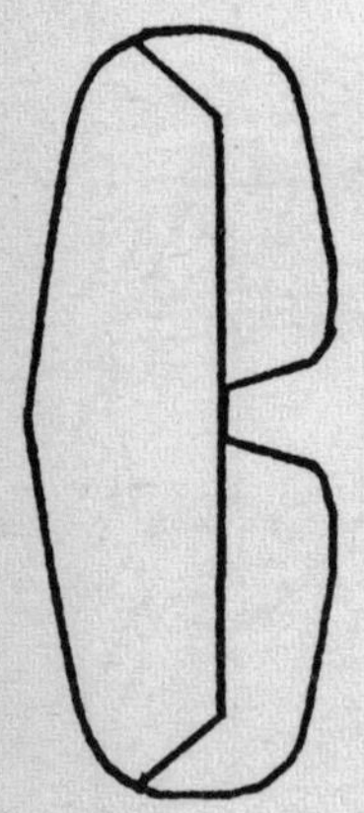

Tailplane. Cut from double thickness or stiffer card.

Propeller blade. Cut three from stiff card or balsa.

Windscreen.

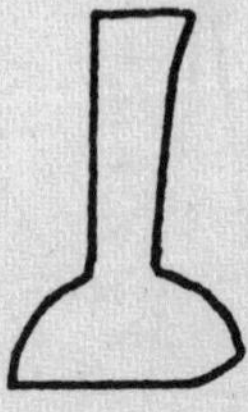

Undercarriage spat. Two required.

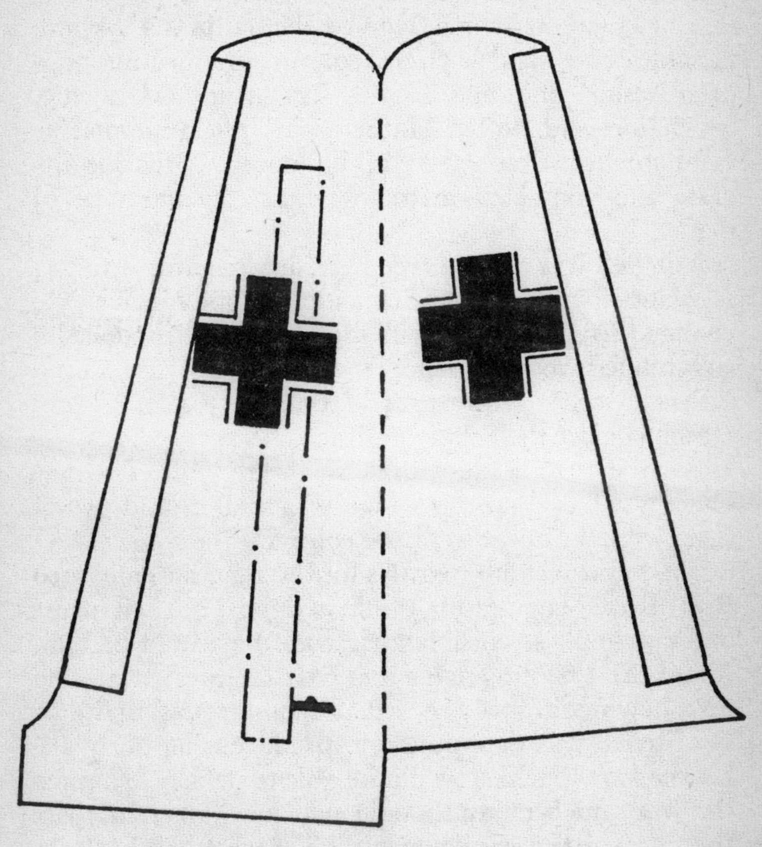

Wing. Two required.

Spitfire

By the time R. J. Mitchell was twenty-five years old he was Chief Designer and Chief Engineer of the Supermarine Aviation Works. He was the son of a Yorkshire Schoolmaster and completed an engineering apprenticeship and had studied Engineering Drawing, Mechanics and Higher Mathematics. The Supermarine Company was concerned with building only marine aircraft and competed in major races for that type of plane.

Mitchell was given a free hand in designing a racing seaplane for the 1925 Schneider Trophy Race. He changed from the usual biplane layout and produced a streamlined wooden monoplane, the *S4,* which set up a seaplane speed record of 226mph (364km/h) but crashed before the Schneider Race.

For the 1927 contest three *S5's* were built. The new plane was based on the *S4* but was smaller and two of them were the only aircraft to complete the course.

Supermarine built two *S6's* for the 1929 race and used Rolls Royce engines for the first time. This new plane had the smallest possible airframes that could be built round the 1,600hp engine and won the race. It also set up a new world speed record at 358mph (574km/h).

Mitchell was determined to produce a fighter plane for the R.A.F. which would be able to defend Britain in the war which many thought was inevitable. In 1936. the first *Spitfire* was flown and plans were laid for large scale production.

The design was based on the experience gained from the Schneider Trophy planes and again a Rolls Royce engine was used. The name *Spitfire* is legendary, and became a household word in 1940 during the Battle of Britain. Several modifications were carried out, more powerful engines fitted and different armament used, and in all, nearly 23,000 examples were built.

Spitfire Mk. V. Fighter **Britain 1941**

Power Rolls Royce Merlin Vee-type engine driving a three-bladed metal propeller 11ft 2in (3.4m) diameter.
Fuselage Armour plated single-seater body 29ft 11in (9.12m) long.
Wings Span 36ft 10in (11.23m).

The normal armament of the *Mk V Spitfire* was two 20mm cannon and four machine guns mounted in the wings.

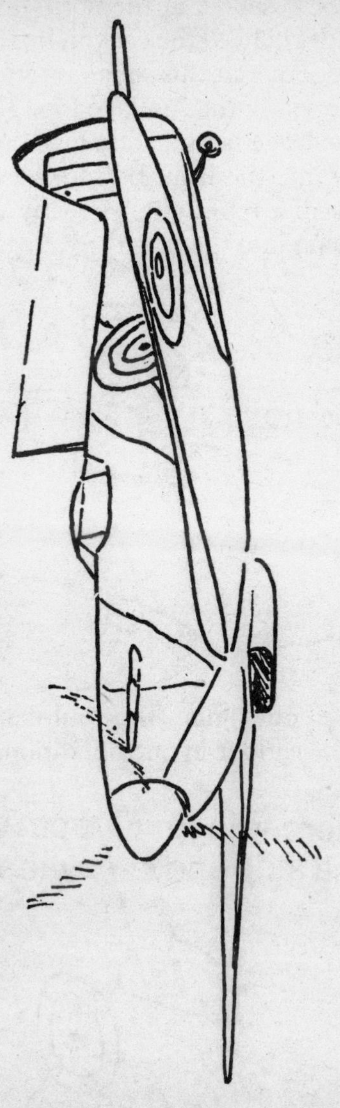

To Make the Spitfire

(1) Cut out the fuselage in the normal way. Glue the bottom to the sides behind the cockpit but do not glue the rudder halves together at this stage. Round the sides and glue the rear section of the fuselage top. The front end is rounded and the large tab glued to give double thickness to this section. Glue the front bottom section into place and when it is dry round the nose by inserting your finger and pressing into the palm of your hand.

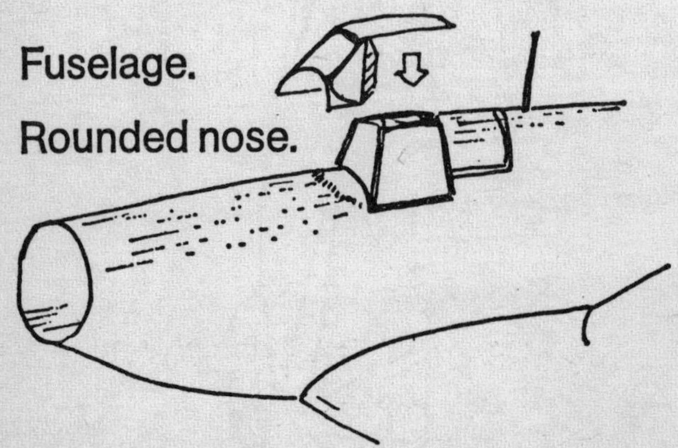

(2) Make up and glue the tailplane in position together with the rudder in one operation.

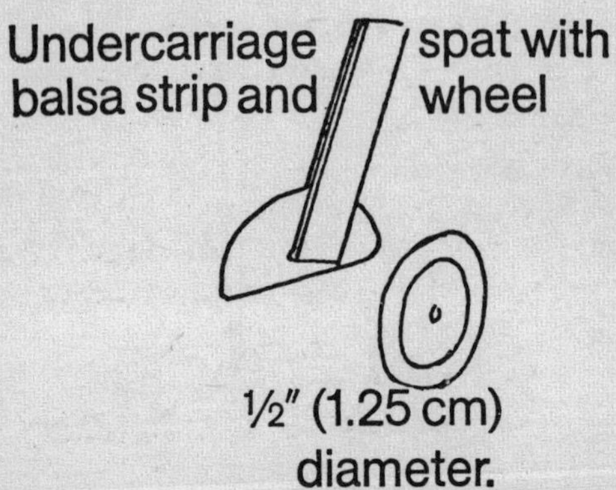

Rear of model showing assembled rudder/tailplane to be glued between rudder sides.

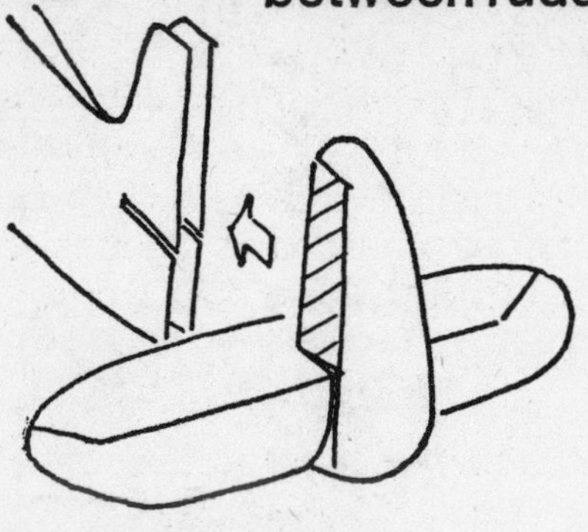

Propeller,
Cut out three from balsa or stiff card.

(3) The wings are both shown and require more than the usual number of balsa strips. The centre strip is double thickness at the fuselage end. Assemble the wings, glue into place and allow to dry.

(4) Cut out the canopy and glue it to the fuselage. Trim a block of soft balsa to fit into the nose and sand it to the shape of the spinner. Add the propeller and undercarriage unless you want to display the model flying.

(5) Paint the underside of the model pale blue and the rest in camouflage dark green and dark brown.

R – Red B – Blue
W – White Y – Yellow

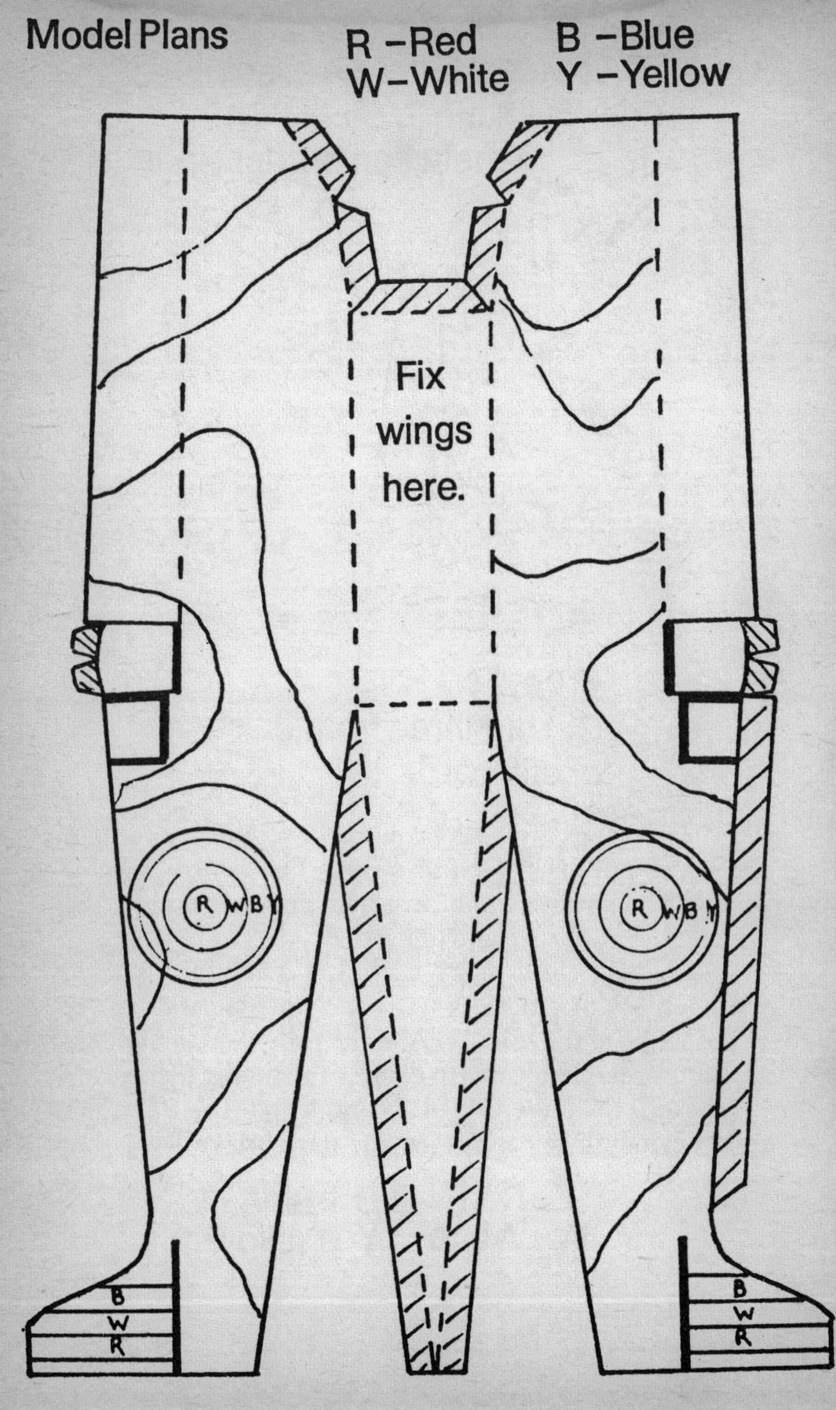
Model Plans
R –Red
W–White
B –Blue
Y –Yellow
Fix wings here.
R W B Y
R W B Y
B
W
R
B
W
R

Windscreen/canopy.

Rudder.

Fuselage front

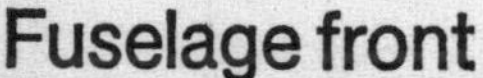

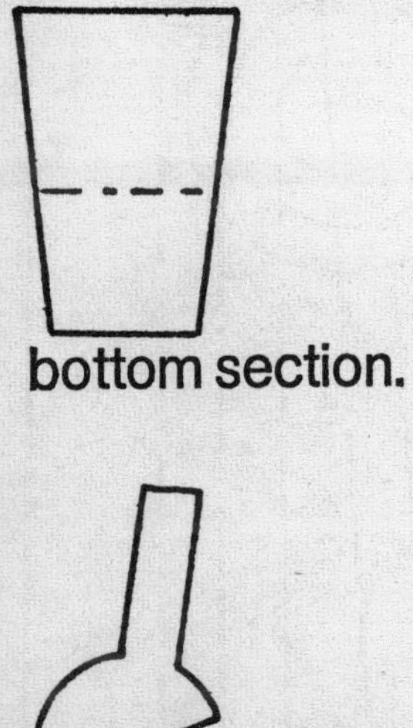

bottom section.

Undercarriage spat.
Cut out two.

Tailplane.
Cut from
thicker card.

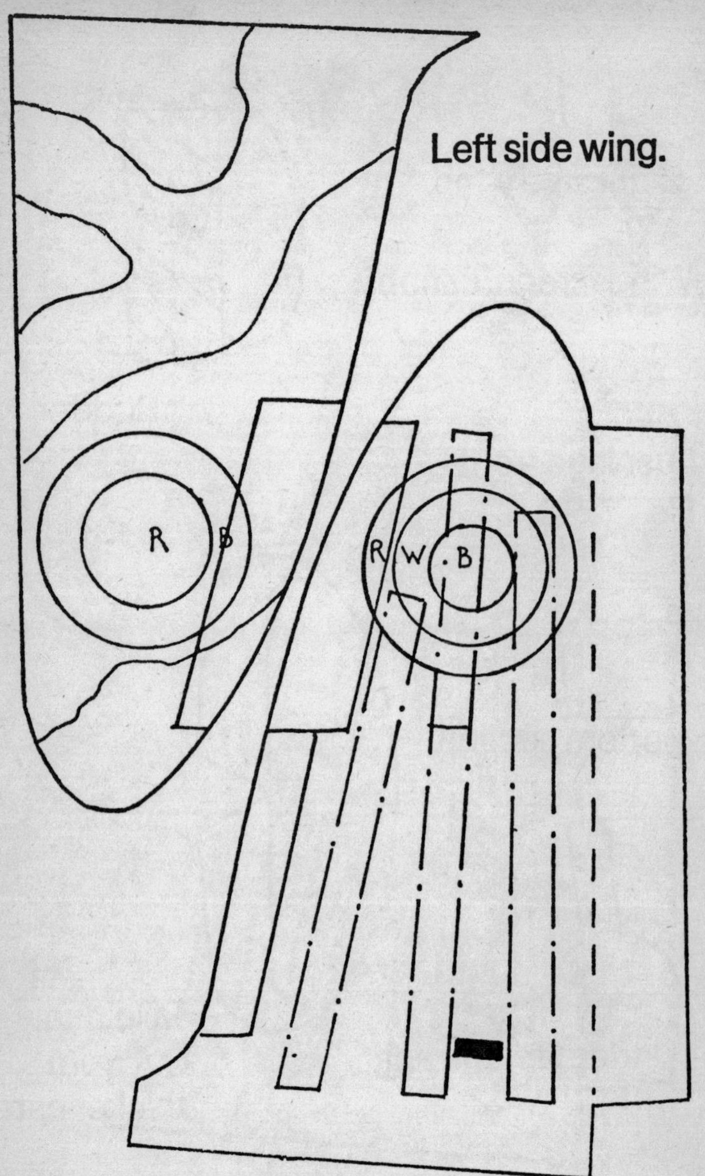

Left side wing.

Right side wing.

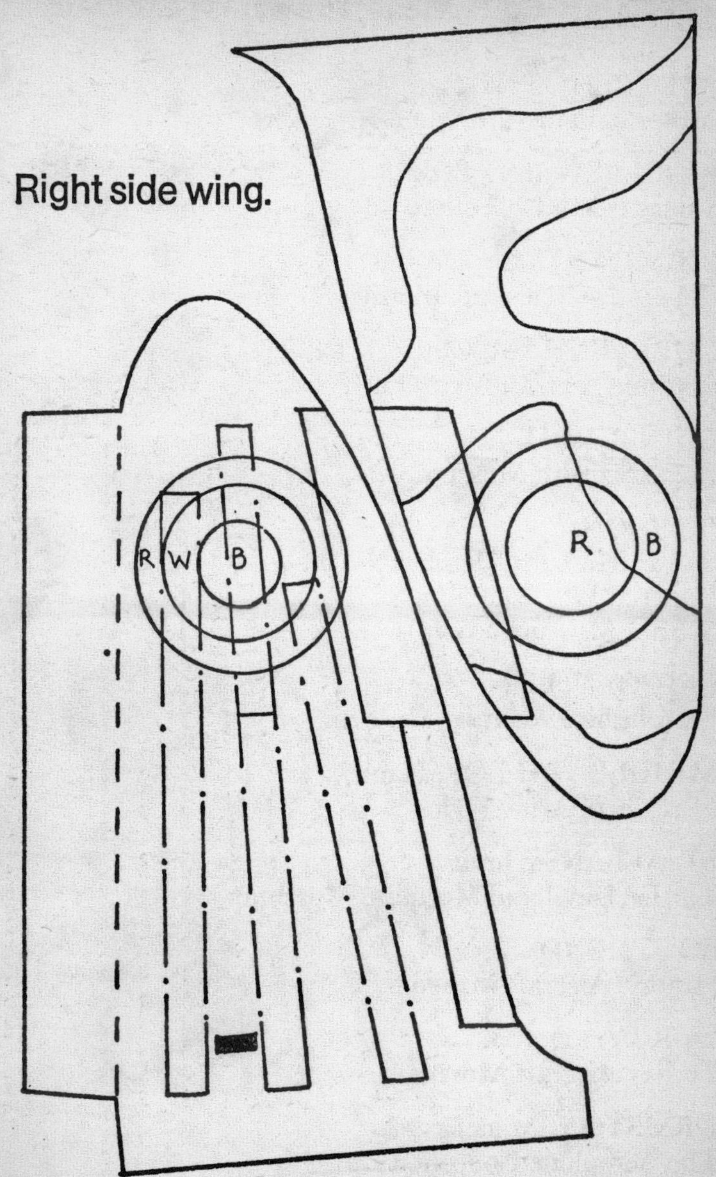

Aircraft Collections That You Can Visit

ALDERSHOT, Hants.
Airborne Forces Museum.

BIGGLESWADE, Beds.
Shuttleworth Collection.

BIRMINGHAM
Museum of Science & Industry.

CHELTENHAM, Glos.
Skyfame Aircraft Museum.

EDINBURGH.
Royal Scottish Museum.

LONDON.
R.A.F. Museum, Hendon NW9.
Imperial War Museum, SE1,
Science Museum SW7.

LINCOLN, Lincs.
Lincolnshire Aviation Museum.

MIDDLE WALLOP, Hants.
Museum of Army Flying.

ST. ALBANS, Herts.
The De Havilland Mosquito Museum.

SOUTHEND, Essex.
Historic Aircraft Museum.

TORBAY, Devon.
Torbay Aircraft Museum.

URMSTON, Manchester.
The Aeroplane Collection Ltd.